Adobe
Acrobat DC

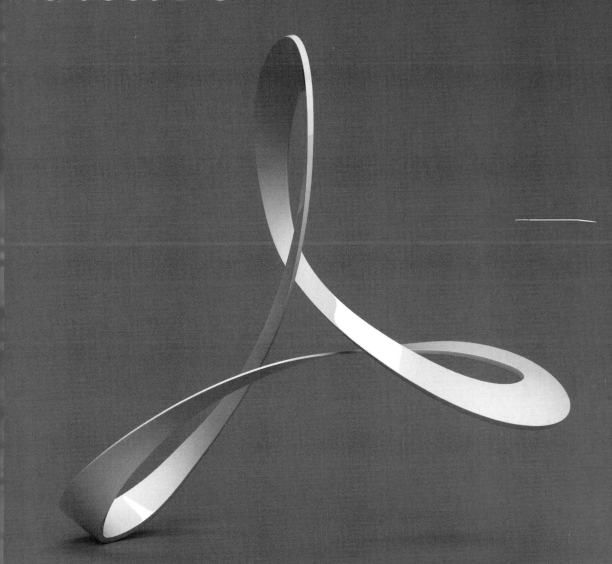

CLASSROOM IN A BOOK®
The official training workbook from Adobe

Lisa Fridsma & Brie Gyncild

ISBN-13:   978-0-134-17183-8

ISBN-10:   0-134-17183-7

9 8 7 6 5 4 3 2 1

WHERE ARE THE LESSON FILES?

Purchasing this Classroom in a Book gives you access to the lesson files you'll need to complete the exercises in the book.

You'll find the files you need on your **Account** page at peachpit.com on the **Lesson & Update Files** tab.

For complete instructions, see "Accessing the Classroom in a Book files" in the Getting Started section of this book.

The example below shows how the files appear on your **Account** page. The files are packaged as ZIP archives, which you will need to expand after downloading. You can download the lessons individually or as a single large ZIP file if your network connection is fast enough.

CONTENTS

GETTING STARTED

Adobe® Acrobat® DC is an essential tool in today's electronic workflow. You can use Acrobat Standard or Acrobat Pro to convert virtually any document to Adobe Portable Document Format (PDF), preserving the exact look and content of the original, complete with fonts and graphics. You can edit text and images in PDF documents, initiate reviews, distribute and share documents, create interactive forms, and more.

About Classroom in a Book

Adobe Acrobat DC Classroom in a Book® is part of the official training series for Adobe graphics and publishing software, developed with the support of Adobe product experts. The lessons are designed to let you learn at your own pace. If you're new to Adobe Acrobat, you'll learn the fundamental concepts and features you'll need to master the program. If you've been using Acrobat for a while, you'll find that Classroom in a Book teaches many advanced features, including tips and techniques for using the newest features. This edition will also help you get up to speed with the completely redesigned Acrobat user interface, so you can find the tools you depend on quickly and easily.

Although each lesson provides step-by-step instructions for working with specific projects, there's room for exploration and experimentation. You can follow the book from start to finish, or do only the lessons that match your interests and needs. Each lesson concludes with a review section summarizing what you've covered.

Acrobat Pro and Acrobat Standard

This book covers features included in Acrobat Pro and Acrobat Standard. We've noted where a tool or feature described in this book is available only in Acrobat Pro. Features available only in Acrobat Pro include:

- Preflighting documents and other print production tasks
- Creating PDF Portfolios
- Checking PDF documents for accessibility
- Applying Bates numbering and redaction
- Comparing versions of a document
- Using and creating actions

Prerequisites

Before beginning to use *Adobe Acrobat DC Classroom in a Book*, you should have a working knowledge of your computer and its operating system. Make sure you know how to use the mouse, standard menus and commands, and also how to open, save, and close files. If you need to review these techniques, see the printed or online documentation included with your system.

Installing Adobe Acrobat

Before beginning to use *Adobe Acrobat DC Classroom in a Book*, make sure that your system is set up correctly and that you've installed the required software and hardware. You must purchase Adobe Acrobat DC software separately. For system requirements, see the Adobe website at www.adobe.com/products/acrobat/main.html.

You must install the application onto your hard drive. Follow the onscreen installation instructions.

Options for purchasing Acrobat DC

Both Acrobat DC Standard and Acrobat DC Pro are available as standalone software and by subscription to Adobe Document Cloud or Adobe Creative Cloud. Which option you choose depends on your individual and organizational needs. However, just as there are feature differences between Acrobat Standard and Acrobat Pro, there are more features available when you have a Document Cloud or Creative Cloud subscription. (While you can purchase a Document Cloud subscription separately, Document Cloud subscriptions are automatically included in Creative Cloud subscriptions.) Where Document Cloud subscriptions are required for a feature, such as using Document Cloud eSign Services, we've noted it in the lessons.

You can learn more and compare your options for purchasing Acrobat DC at acrobat.adobe.com/us/en/pricing/pricing-compare-plans.html.

Starting Adobe Acrobat

You start Acrobat just as you would any other software application.

- **Windows:** Choose Start > Programs or All Programs > Adobe Acrobat DC.
- **Mac OS:** Open the Adobe Acrobat DC folder, and double-click the program icon.

Accessing the Classroom in a Book files

The lessons in *Adobe Acrobat DC Classroom in a Book* use specific source files. To complete the lessons in this book, you need to download the lesson files from peachpit.com. You can download the files for individual lessons, or download them all in a single file.

Your Account page is also where you'll find any updates to the chapters or to the lesson files. Look on the Lesson & Update Files tab to access the most current content.

To access the Classroom in a Book files, do the following:

1 On a desktop or laptop computer, go to www.peachpit.com/redeem, and enter the code found at the back of your book.

2 If you do not have a Peachpit.com account, create one when you're prompted to do so.

3 Click the Lesson & Update Files tab on your Account page. This tab lists downloadable files for all Peachpit and Adobe Press products you have purchased and registered.

4 Click the lesson file links to download them to your computer, and then unzip them.

The files are compressed into zip archives to speed up download time and to protect the contents from damage during transfer. You must uncompress (or "unzip") the files to restore them to their original size and format before you use them with the book. On a modern operating system, simply double-click a zip archive to open it.

5 Create a new folder on your hard disk, and name it **Lessons**. Then, drag the lesson files you downloaded and uncompressed into the Lessons folder on your hard disk.

When you begin each lesson, you will navigate to the folder with that lesson number, where you will find all of the project files you need to complete the lesson.

● **Note:** As you complete each lesson, you will preserve the start files. In case you overwrite them, you can restore the original files by downloading the corresponding lesson files from your Account page at peachpit.com.

Additional resources

Adobe Acrobat DC Classroom in a Book is not meant to replace documentation provided that comes with the program or to be a comprehensive reference for every feature. Only the commands and options used in the lessons are explained in this book. For comprehensive information about program features and tutorials, refer to these resources:

• **Adobe Acrobat Learn and Support:** helpx.adobe.com/acrobat.html has comprehensive content you can search or browse, provided by Adobe. This includes hands-on tutorials, a link to Help, answers to common questions, troubleshooting information, and more.

• **Adobe Acrobat DC Help:** helpx.adobe.com/acrobat/topics.html is a reference for application features, commands, and tools (press F1 or choose Help > Online Support). You can also download Help as a PDF document optimized for printing at helpx.adobe.com/pdf/acrobat_reference.pdf.

- **Acrobat Forums:** forums.adobe.com/community/acrobat lets you tap into peer-to-peer discussions and questions and answers on Acrobat and other Adobe products.

- **Adobe Creative Cloud Learn:** helpx.adobe.com/support.html provides inspiration, key techniques, cross-product workflows, and updates on new features.

- **Resources for educators:** www.adobe.com/education and edex.adobe.com offer a treasure trove of information for instructors who teach classes on Adobe software. Find solutions for education at all levels, including free curricula that use an integrated approach to teaching Adobe software and can be used to prepare for the Adobe Certified Associate exams.

Also check out these useful links:

- **Adobe Add-ons:** creative.adobe.com/addons is a central resource for finding tools, services, extensions, code samples, and more to supplement and extend your Adobe products.

- **Adobe Acrobat DC product home page:** www.adobe.com/products/acrobat has more information about the product.

Adobe Authorized Training Centers

Adobe Authorized Training Centers offer instructor-led courses and training on Adobe products. A directory of AATCs is available at partners.adobe.com.

Going mobile

The free Adobe Acrobat DC mobile app makes it easy to view and work with PDF files from anywhere on your Android and iOS devices (including iPad, iPhone, and iPod touch). With the free app, you can view PDF files; add comments using the highlight, strikethrough, underline, and freehand drawing tools; view password-protected and encrypted PDF files; and fill out, save, and send fillable PDF forms. You can even sign forms with your finger using the Ink Signature tool.

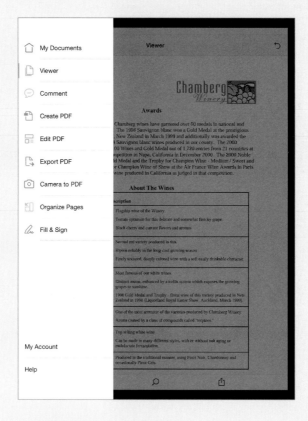

With a Document Cloud or Creative Cloud subscription, the app becomes more powerful. You can use it to create, export, and organize pages in a PDF file. If you're working on an iPad, you can also edit pages in a PDF document.

You can download the app free from iTunes or the Apple App Store (for iPad, iPhone, or iPod touch), from Google play (for Android), or from the Windows Phone Store (for Windows Phone).

For more information about the Acrobat DC mobile app, visit acrobat.adobe.com/us/en/products/mobile-app.html.

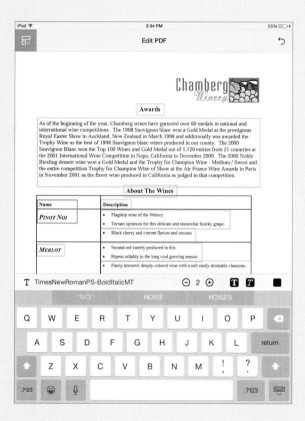

1 INTRODUCING ADOBE ACROBAT DC

Lesson overview

In this lesson, you'll do the following:

- Get acquainted with the Portable Document Format (PDF), Acrobat DC, and Acrobat Reader DC.

- Select tools in the toolbars.

- Use tools in the Tools pane.

- Customize toolbars.

- Navigate a PDF document using the toolbars, menu commands, page thumbnails, and bookmarks.

- Change the view of a document in the document pane.

- View a PDF document in Read mode.

- Learn to use Adobe Acrobat DC Help.

 This lesson will take approximately an hour to complete. Copy the Lesson01 folder onto your hard drive if you haven't already done so.

The Acrobat DC workspace puts the tools you need at your fingertips without cluttering up the screen. You can customize the toolbars for quicker access to tools you use frequently.

About PDF

Portable Document Format (PDF) is a file format that preserves all of the fonts, formatting, colors, and graphics of any source document, regardless of the application and platform used to create the original document. PDF files are compact and secure. Anyone using the free Acrobat Reader DC can view, navigate, comment on, and print a PDF file. Acrobat Reader users can also complete and return PDF forms and electronically sign PDF documents.

- PDF preserves the exact layout, fonts, and text formatting of electronic documents, regardless of the computer system or platform used to view these documents.

- You can read PDF documents using Acrobat Reader, Acrobat Standard, or Acrobat Pro.

- PDF documents can contain multiple languages, such as Japanese and English, on the same page.

- PDF documents print predictably, with proper margins and page breaks.

- You can secure PDF files to prevent unauthorized changes or printing or to limit access to confidential documents.

- You can change the view magnification of a PDF page in Acrobat or Acrobat Reader, which is especially useful for zooming in on graphics or diagrams containing intricate details.

- You can share your PDF files using network and web servers, email, CDs, DVDs, other removable media, and the Document Cloud.

About Adobe Acrobat

Adobe Acrobat lets you create, manage, edit, assemble, and search PDF documents. Additionally, you can create forms, initiate review processes, apply legal features, and prepare PDF documents for professional printing.

Almost any document—a text file, a file created in a page-layout or graphics application, a scanned document, a web page, or a digital photo—can be converted to Adobe PDF using Acrobat software or third-party authoring applications. Your workflow and document type determine the best way to create a PDF.

About Acrobat Reader

Acrobat Reader, available free online, is the global standard for viewing PDF files. It is the only PDF viewer that can open and interact with all PDF documents. Acrobat Reader makes it possible to view, search, digitally sign, verify, print, and collaborate on PDF files without having Acrobat installed.

Acrobat Reader can natively display rich media content, including video and audio files. You can also view PDF Portfolios in Acrobat Reader.

By default, Acrobat Reader for Windows opens PDF files in Protected Mode (known as "sandboxing" to IT professionals). In Protected Mode, Reader confines any processes to the application itself, so that potentially malicious PDF files do not have access to your computer and its system files. To verify that Acrobat Reader is in Protected Mode, choose File > Properties, select the Advanced tab, and view the Protected Mode status.

About the Acrobat DC mobile app

The Adobe Acrobat DC mobile app lets you work with PDF files on tablets and phones. This book introduces you to the features in the desktop version of Acrobat, some of which are available in the mobile app. To learn more about the mobile app, see "Going mobile" on page 6.

Using PDF on the web

The web has greatly expanded the possibilities for delivering electronic documents to a wide and varied audience. Because web browsers can be configured to run other applications inside the browser window, you can post PDF files as part of a website. Visitors to your site can download or view these PDF files inside the browser window using Acrobat Reader.

When including a PDF file as part of your web page, consider directing users to the Adobe website so that the first time they encounter a PDF, they can download Acrobat Reader, free of charge, if necessary.

PDFs can be viewed one page at a time and printed from the web. With page-at-a-time downloading, the web server sends only the requested page, decreasing downloading time. In addition, you can easily print selected pages or all pages from the document. PDF is a suitable format for publishing long electronic documents on the web, and PDF documents print predictably, with proper margins and page breaks.

You can also download and convert web pages to PDF, making it easy to save, distribute, and print them. (For more information, see Lesson 2, "Creating Adobe PDF Files.")

Adding Acrobat Reader installers

Acrobat Reader is available free of charge, making it easier for users to view your PDF documents. You can point users to the Acrobat Reader installers on the Adobe website at www.adobe.com. If you're distributing documents on a CD or DVD, you can include a copy of the Acrobat Reader installers on the disc.

If you're including the Acrobat Reader installers on a disc, you should include a ReadMe text file at the top level of the CD or DVD that describes how to install Acrobat Reader and provides any last-minute information.

You may make and distribute unlimited copies of Acrobat Reader, including copies for commercial distribution. For complete information on distributing and giving your users access to Acrobat Reader, visit the Adobe website at www.adobe.com/products/reader/distribution.html.

A special logo is available from Adobe for use when distributing Acrobat Reader.

Opening a PDF file

The default Acrobat DC work area is streamlined to ensure easy access to the tools you'll use most often as you work with PDF files.

1 Start Acrobat.

The Acrobat Home screen lists files you've recently opened or files you've sent to others. You want to open a file you haven't opened before, so it's not in the list of recent files.

▶ **Tip:** If you close the menu bar by choosing View > Show/Hide > Menu Bar, you won't be able to access any menu commands to reopen it. To reopen the menu bar, press F9 (Windows) or Command+Shift+M (Mac OS) on your keyboard.

2 Click My Computer in the Storage area on the left.

3 Click Browse, navigate to the Lesson01 folder on your hard drive, and select the Conference Guide.pdf file.

4   Click Open.

The menu bar and a toolbar are visible at the top of the work area. In Acrobat DC, each open document has its own work area and toolbars. You can access common commands in the menu bar.

▶ **Tip:** In Windows, you can move between open PDF documents by clicking a file's icon in the Windows Taskbar.

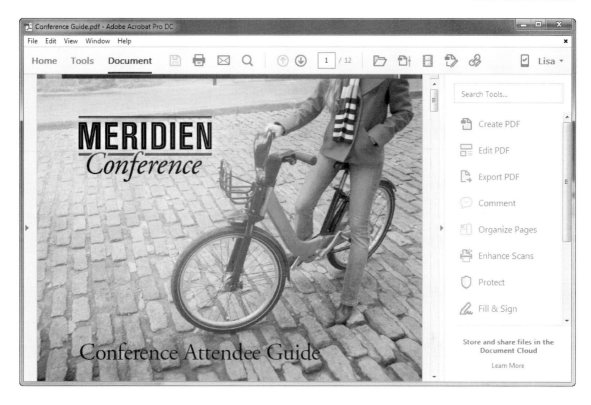

Acrobat can open in two different ways—as a standalone application or in a web browser. The associated work areas differ in small but important ways. This book assumes that you are using Acrobat as a standalone application.

5   Move your pointer down to the lower left corner of the document window to reveal the size of this page. (The document window is the part of the workspace that displays an open document.) The page size display disappears when you move the pointer away from the area.

Working with toolbars

The main Acrobat toolbar contains commonly used tools and commands for working with PDF files. You can show additional tools in the toolbar, add tools to the Quick Tools portion of the toolbar, and show recently used tools. The toolbar is designed to be simple and streamlined, giving you the control to add only the tools you use frequently.

Using the toolbar

By default, the toolbar includes the Home, Tools, and Document buttons; buttons for saving, printing, or emailing a PDF file; the Find Text tool, and a few navigation tools, such as the Next Page tool. To use a tool, click it.

To see the name or description of a tool in the toolbar, hover the pointer over the tool.

Using the Page Controls toolbar

In addition to the main toolbar, you can access tools from the Page Controls toolbar that appears when you hover the mouse over the bottom of the screen. In that toolbar, you can select the Selection and Hand tools, change the page magnification, show or hide thumbnails, and select a page view option. You can also dock the page controls to the main toolbar.

You'll use the Page Controls toolbar to navigate the page.

1   Move the mouse to the bottom of the screen until you see the Page Controls toolbar. Click the Zoom In button (⊕) three times.

Acrobat enlarges the view. Only part of the document appears in the application window.

2 Click the Hand tool (✋) in the Page Controls toolbar.

The default tool in Acrobat is the Selection tool (▶). The Hand tool lets you pan around the document.

3 With the Hand tool selected, drag the document across the application window to see a different portion of the image.

4 Click the Zoom Out button (⊖) once to see more of the page.

The Zoom tools do not change the actual size of a document. They change only its magnification on your screen.

5 Click the arrow to the right of the magnification text box, and choose Fit Visible from the pop-up menu to display the entire page.

▶ Tip: An arrow to the right of a tool indicates that there is a menu associated with that tool. Click the arrow to reveal that menu.

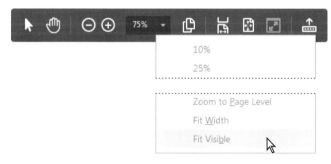

Working with tools

The commands and options you need in order to perform different tasks are grouped in the Tools pane on the right side of the application window. Additional tools are available in the Tools Center; you can access them directly from the Tools Center or add them to the Tools pane. When you select a tool, the user interface changes to provide the options related to that tool.

Selecting tools in the Tools pane

To become familiar with using tools, you'll rotate a page and edit some text.

1   Click Organize Pages in the Tools pane on the right side of the screen.

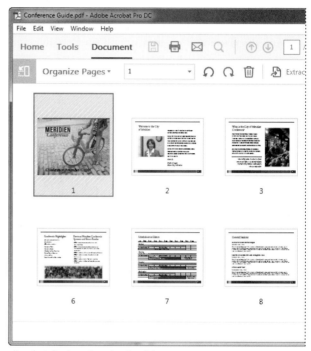

Select Organize Pages in the Tools pane

Acrobat displays thumbnails of the pages

Acrobat displays thumbnail previews of each of the pages in the document, with page numbers shown beneath them. The Organize Pages toolbar appears below the main Acrobat toolbar.

2   Click the page 9 thumbnail. Three blue icons appear over the selected thumbnail: two rotation icons and a trash icon.

The map of Meridien on page 9 is oriented incorrectly. You'll correct it.

3   Click the clockwise rotation icon.

The page rotates to the correct orientation, and no other pages are affected.

4   Click the X at the end of the Organize Pages toolbar to return to the main document view.

5   Click Edit PDF in the Tools pane.

The Edit PDF toolbar appears below the main Acrobat toolbar. On the right side of the application window, a pane displays options related to editing text and images. The document window displays the current page. By default, Edit is selected in the Edit PDF toolbar.

When you select a tool, the user interface changes to show you the options and content you need to effectively use that tool. How it changes varies from tool to tool.

6   In the main toolbar, type **12** in the page number box, and then press Enter or Return to go to that page.

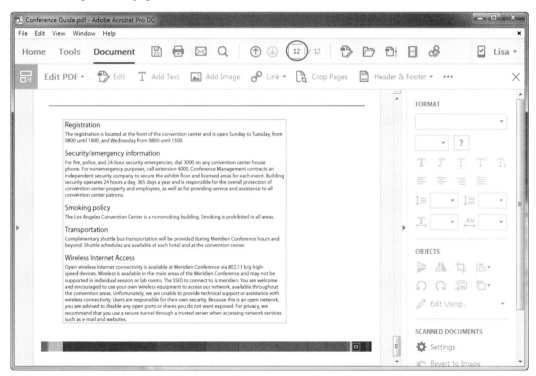

Because Edit is selected in the Edit PDF toolbar, editable content is outlined on the page. A box appears around the text. The pointer changes to an I-beam when you move it over the text.

Tools in the Tools pane

By default, the Tools pane displays the most commonly used tools. To add or remove a tool from the pane, click Tools in the main toolbar to open the Tools Center view. Then choose Add Shortcut or Remove Shortcut from the menu beneath a tool. Acrobat uses the current Tools pane configuration in all PDF documents you open until you change the configuration again. (Some of the tools are available only in Acrobat Pro.)

These tools are included in the Tools pane by default:

- Create PDF: Create a PDF file from almost any file or scanned image.
- Edit PDF: Edit text, images, links, and other content, and crop pages.
- Export PDF: Export PDF files as Microsoft Office documents, images, HTML web pages, and other formats.
- Comments: Add, search, read, reply to, import, and export comments.
- Organize Pages: Rotate, delete, insert, replace, split, extract, and otherwise manipulate pages.
- Enhance Scans: Make text editable, and otherwise improve the quality of scanned documents.
- Protect: Apply security features such as file encryption.
- Fill & Sign: Complete and sign forms electronically.
- Prepare Form: Create and edit PDF forms.
- Send For Signature: Request signatures from others, and track results.
- Send & Track: Share documents with others, and track views and downloads.

7   Select the word *and* in the second sentence of the Wireless Internet Access topic.

8   Type **but** to replace the word *and*.

● **Note:** If the original font is not available, Acrobat substitutes a default font and displays a tool tip informing you that the font has been substituted.

Conference via 802.11 b/g high-Meridien Conference and may not be hnect to is meridien. You are welcome ess our network, available throughout de technical support or assistance with urity. Because this is an open network, ot want exposed. For privacy, we erver when accessing network services

Conference via 802.11 b/g high-Meridien Conference but may not be hnect to is meridien. You are welcome ess our network, available throughout de technical support or assistance with urity. Because this is an open network, ot want exposed. For privacy, we erver when accessing network services

9 From the pop-up menu at the left side of the Edit PDF toolbar, choose Back To Document to close the Edit PDF tool.

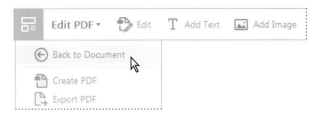

10 Choose File > Save As.

11 Navigate to the Lesson01 folder, name the file **Conference Guide_final.pdf**, and click Save. Leave the file open.

Navigating PDF documents

You can zoom in and out, move to different pages, show multiple pages at a time, view multiple documents, and even split a document to view different areas of the same document simultaneously. Many navigation tools are available in more than one place; you can use the method that best suits your workflow.

Changing magnification

Earlier in this lesson, you used the Zoom In and Zoom Out tools, as well as the Preset Magnification menu, all in the Page Controls toolbar. You can also change the magnification using commands in the View menu.

1 Choose File > Open, navigate to the Meridien Rev.pdf file in the Lesson01 folder, and click Open.

2 Choose View > Zoom > Fit Height.

The entire PDF document is displayed, fitting the height of the application window.

3 Choose View > Zoom > Zoom To.

4 In the Zoom To dialog box, type **125%** for Magnification, and then click OK.

Accessing specific pages

You've used the page number text box in the Acrobat toolbar to go to a specific page. You can also use commands in the View menu or use the Page Thumbnails panel in the navigation pane to quickly move to a different page in the document.

1 Choose Window > Conference Guide_final.pdf to display the file you worked with earlier. If the Conference Guide_final.pdf file isn't open, open it.

2 Choose View > Page Navigation > Go To Page.

3 In the Go To Page dialog box, type **7**, and click OK.

 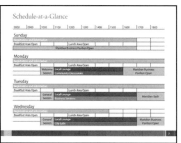

Acrobat displays page 7 of the document.

4 Choose View > Page Navigation > Previous Page.

Acrobat displays page 6 of the document. The Previous Page and Next Page commands serve the same purpose as the Previous Page and Next Page buttons in the Acrobat toolbar.

5 If the navigation pane isn't visible, click the arrow on the left side of the application window to open it.

6 In the navigation pane, click the Page Thumbnails button ( ).

Acrobat displays thumbnails of all the pages in the document. Acrobat automatically creates thumbnails for the pages of a PDF document when you open it.

7 Click the thumbnail for page 3.

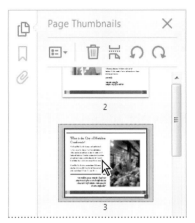

Acrobat displays page 3 of the document.

8 Zoom in to 200%. Notice that the thumbnail highlights the area of the page that is visible at this magnification.

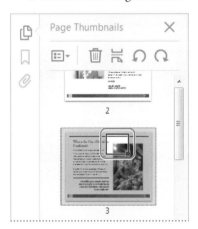

9 Select the Hand tool (🖐) in the Page Controls toolbar.

10 Drag in the document window to see a different area of the page. Notice that the highlighted area in the thumbnail moves accordingly.

Using bookmarks to navigate documents

You can create bookmarks to help viewers navigate PDF documents. Bookmarks act as an electronic table of contents page, providing links directly to the content they describe.

1   Click the Bookmarks button (□) directly below the Page Thumbnails button in the navigation pane.

Acrobat displays the bookmarks that have been created for this PDF document.

2   Click the Meridien Wi-Fi bookmark.

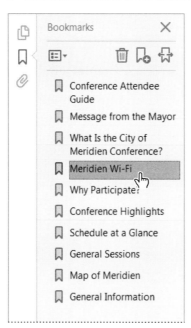

Acrobat displays page 4, which contains information about Meridien wireless access.

▶ **Tip:** You can create bookmarks for a PDF document in Acrobat, or you can generate them automatically when you create the PDF using PDFMaker or when you export a PDF file from InDesign.

3   Click the General Sessions bookmark.

Acrobat displays page 8, where the descriptions of the conference sessions begin. You do not need to create a bookmark for each page.

4   Click the General Information bookmark.

Acrobat displays page 10, where the general information begins. You'll create another bookmark to help conference attendees locate information about accessing first aid quickly.

5   Click the Next Page button (⊕) in the Acrobat toolbar to go to page 11.

6   Select the Selection tool (🖈) in the Page Controls toolbar, and then select the "First aid information" heading on the page.

7   Click the New Bookmark button (🔖) at the top of the Bookmarks panel.

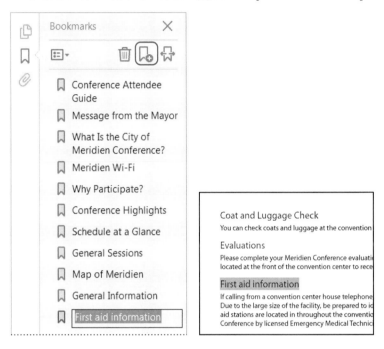

Acrobat adds a new bookmark with the text you selected beneath the General Information bookmark.

8   Drag the new bookmark over the General Information bookmark (directly over the words "General Information") until you see a small triangle, and then release the mouse button.

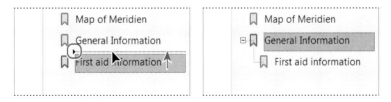

Acrobat indents the new bookmark, nesting it under the General Information bookmark.

Viewing multiple documents

You can work with more than one PDF file at a time, displaying the documents vertically or horizontally. You've opened two PDF documents; you'll view them next to each other.

1 Choose Window > Tile > Vertically.

Acrobat displays all the open PDF files side by side. Notice that each document has its own application window, complete with toolbars and panes.

2 Choose Window > Tile > Horizontally.

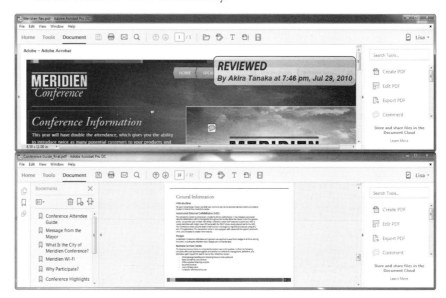

Acrobat displays the PDF documents in their own application windows once again, but this time they're displayed horizontally.

3 Choose Window > Cascade.

Acrobat displays the active document in front of the others, but you can see the title bar for each of the other open documents.

Splitting the view of a document

Sometimes you need to work with different portions of a single document simultaneously, whether it's to ensure you've used consistent wording or to examine differences in images. You can split a document into two views, with the ability to navigate each individually.

1   Click the Conference Guide_final.pdf file to make it active, and then choose Window > Split.

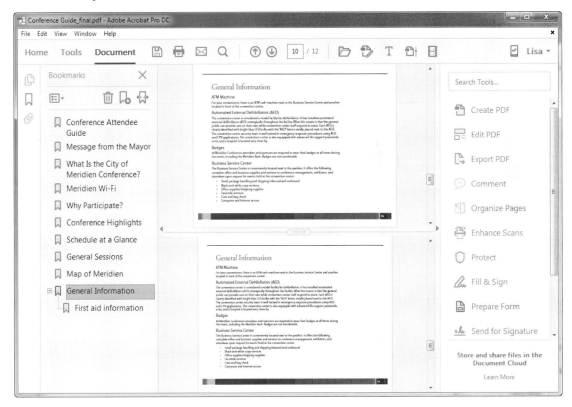

Acrobat displays the same document twice, each with its own scroll bar. Notice that both copies of the document share the same toolbars and panes.

2   Click anywhere in the top version of the document. It's now the active view.

3   Click the Previous Page button to go to the previous page in the top view. Only the top view changes.

4   Click anywhere in the bottom view to make it active.

5   Zoom in to 150%. Only the bottom view changes.

6   Choose Window > Remove Split.

Acrobat restores the document to a single view, displaying whichever view was active when you chose the Remove Split command.

7   Close all open documents without saving changes.

Viewing PDF presentations in Full Screen mode

You can set up a PDF file to be viewed in Full Screen mode, or choose to view any document that way. In Full Screen mode, the menu bar and toolbars are hidden.

1　Choose File > Open, and double-click the Aquo_Financial.pdf file, located in the Lesson01 folder.

2　Click Yes in the Full Screen message box to open this document in Full Screen mode.

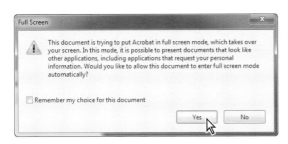

Notice that in Full Screen mode the document occupies all available space on the monitor. All the Acrobat toolbars, menus, and panes have disappeared.

This document is an informational presentation, designed to be viewed exclusively onscreen. The graphics, large type size, and horizontal page layout have been designed for optimal display on a monitor.

You can view any PDF file in Full Screen mode by opening the document in Acrobat and choosing View > Full Screen Mode.

3　Press Enter or Return to page through the presentation. You can also use the arrow keys on your keyboard to move forward and backward.

4　Press the Esc key to exit Full Screen mode.

5　To ensure that navigation controls are always accessible to you, even in Full Screen mode, choose Edit > Preferences (Windows) or Acrobat > Preferences (Mac OS), and select Full Screen from the list of categories in the Preferences dialog box. Select the Show Navigation Bar option, and click OK to apply your changes.

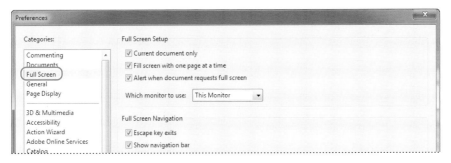

From this point on, whenever you open a document in Acrobat on your computer in Full Screen mode, Acrobat will display Next Page, Previous Page, and Exit Full Screen View buttons at the bottom left of the document window. The buttons appear when you first view the document in Full Screen mode, and then disappear so that they don't obstruct the presentation. To access the buttons, move the pointer over the lower left corner of the screen. Keep in mind that Full Screen viewing preferences are specific to the computer on which you run a PDF presentation, not to
the document.

To set a file to open in Full Screen mode, choose File > Properties, click the Initial View tab in the Document Properties dialog box, select Open In Full Screen Mode, and click OK. Then save the document. For more information, see Lesson 4, "Enhancing PDF Documents."

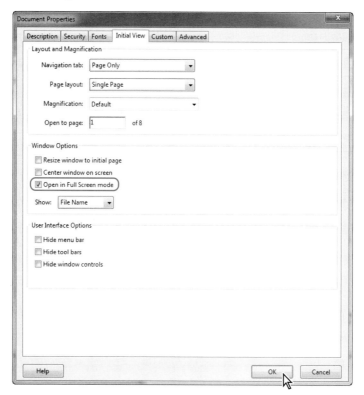

Viewing PDF files in Read mode

You can maximize the screen space available to your PDF document without entering Full Screen mode. Read mode hides all the elements of the work area except the document and the menu bar.

1 Choose View > Read Mode.

2 Move the pointer near the bottom of the window.

A floating toolbar appears briefly when you move the pointer near the bottom of the page. This floating toolbar, which is different from the Page Controls toolbar, includes navigational tools that let you zoom in and out, move to different pages, and save or print the file.

3 To restore the work area, click the Show Main Toolbar button (▣) in the floating toolbar, or choose View > Read Mode again.

4 Choose File > Close, and close the file without saving any changes.

Setting Acrobat preferences for web browsing

You can set the Acrobat Internet preferences to determine how Acrobat loads and displays PDF files from the Internet.

In Acrobat, choose Edit > Preferences (Windows) or Acrobat > Preferences (Mac OS), and select Internet from the categories on the left. By default, several Internet preference options are automatically selected.

- **Display In Read Mode By Default** displays PDF files without toolbars or panes, so that all that appears is a semi-transparent floating toolbar when you move your mouse over the lower area of the PDF file. If you deselect this option, PDF files open with toolbars and panes.

- **Allow Fast Web View** downloads PDF documents for viewing on the web one page at a time. If this option is not selected, the entire PDF file downloads before it is displayed.

- **Allow Speculative Downloading In The Background** enables a PDF document to continue downloading from the web, even after the first requested page displays. Downloading in the background stops when any other task, such as paging through the document, is initiated in Acrobat.

For help setting up your browser to enable you to view PDF documents in it, click the link at the top of the Web Browser Options area of the Preferences dialog box to see instructions.

Customizing the Acrobat toolbar

Note: You can add and remove tools to the right of the Edit Current Tool Set button in the Quick Tools toolbar, but you cannot move or remove anything to its left, such as the Save and Print buttons.

The Acrobat toolbar includes a few commonly used tools by default. You can add tools you use frequently through the Show/Hide commands or by adding them to the Quick Tools section of the toolbar. Changes you make to the toolbar are application-wide, so the toolbar appears the same in any PDF file (until you change the toolbar settings again).

1 Open any document in Acrobat so that you have access to the toolbars.

2 Choose View > Show/Hide > Toolbar Items > Show Page Navigation Tools > Previous View.

The Previous View button appears in the toolbar, just to the left of the page number.

3 Choose View > Show/Hide > Toolbar Items > Show Edit Tools > Undo.

The Undo button appears in the toolbar, next to the Find button. You may have noticed that the Show/Hide options add commands from the File, Edit, and View menus to the toolbar, positioned in the toolbar according to their menu and sub-menu (such as Page Navigation).

The Quick Tools area of the toolbar contains tools you add through the Tools pane. Almost every tool is available.

4 Choose View > Show/Hide > Toolbar Items > Customize Quick Tools.

The Customize Quick Tools dialog box opens. The tools currently in the Quick Tools toolbar are displayed across the top of the dialog box. Tools you can add are listed below. You'll add the Rotate Left and Rotate Right tools to the toolbar.

5 Click Organize Pages to expand it.

6 Select the Left tool (⟳), and then click the Add To Toolbar button (⟲↑) to add the tool to the set at the top.

7 Select the Right tool (⟳), and then click the Add To Toolbar button.

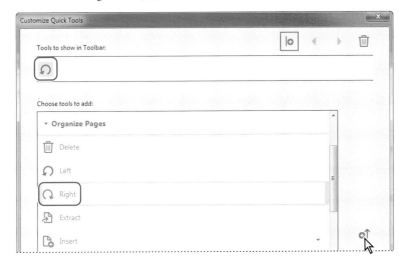

8 Click Organize Pages to collapse the section again, and then click Create PDF to expand it.

9 Select PDF From File, and click the Add To Toolbar button.

You've added three buttons to the Quick Tools area of the toolbar. You can rearrange tools, add dividers to organize them visually, and delete tools.

10 With the PDF From File tool still selected, click the left arrow button at the top of the dialog box twice to move it to left of the rotation tools.

11 Click the Add Divider button at the top of the dialog box to add a divider between the PDF From File tool and the rotation tools.

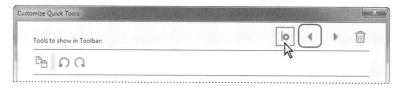

▶ **Tip:** To automatically add the tools you use frequently to the toolbar, choose View > Show/Hide > Toolbar Items > Show Recently Used Tools.

When you click the Add Divider button, Acrobat inserts a divider immediately after the currently selected tool. You can move a divider just as you move a tool, using the right and left arrow buttons at the top of the dialog box.

12 Click Save to save your changes.

The tools and divider you added appear on the right end of the toolbar.

Getting help

The lessons in this book focus on commonly used tools and features in Acrobat DC. However, you can get complete information on all the Acrobat tools, commands, and features for both Windows and Mac OS systems from Adobe Acrobat DC Help online. To access Help, choose Help > Online Support. Acrobat opens your default browser and displays the Acrobat Help page online.

If you do not have an Internet connection, Acrobat displays a message suggesting you verify your Internet connection. If you plan to work in Acrobat without an Internet connection, you can download the Acrobat Help topics as a PDF document from the Adobe Acrobat DC Help And Support page, and then open and search the PDF file as you would any other.

In addition to the Help topics, the Acrobat Help page also provides links to tutorials to help you learn Acrobat, user forums, and other community resources related to Adobe Acrobat.

Review questions

1 Name two advantages of PDF documents.

2 How do you navigate to a different page in Acrobat?

3 How do you access the Page Controls toolbar?

4 How can you return to your usual work area from Full Screen mode?

Review answers

1 PDF provides several advantages, including the following:

- PDF preserves the exact layout, fonts, and text formatting of electronic documents, regardless of the computer system or platform used to view these documents.

- PDF documents can contain multiple languages, such as Japanese and English, on the same page.

- PDF documents print predictably, with proper margins and page breaks.

- You can secure PDF files to prevent unauthorized changes or printing, or to limit access to confidential documents.

- You can change the view magnification of a PDF page in Acrobat or Acrobat Reader, which is especially useful for zooming in on graphics or diagrams containing intricate details.

2 To navigate to a different page, you can do any of the following:

- Click the Next Page or Previous Page button in the Acrobat toolbar.

- Type a page number in the Acrobat toolbar.

- Choose a command from the View > Page Navigation menu.

- Click a thumbnail in the Page Thumbnails panel in the navigation pane.

- Click a bookmark in the Bookmarks panel in the navigation pane.

3 To access the Page Controls toolbar, move your cursor over the bottom of the application window.

4 To exit Full Screen mode and return to your normal work area, press the Esc key on your keyboard.

2 CREATING ADOBE PDF FILES

Lesson overview

In this lesson, you'll do the following:

- Convert a TIFF file to Adobe PDF using the Create PDF tool.

- Convert a file to Adobe PDF using the authoring application's Print command.

- Convert multiple documents into a single PDF file.

- Explore the Adobe PDF settings used to convert files to Adobe PDF.

- Reduce the size of a PDF file.

- Scan a paper document into Acrobat.

- Convert scanned images into searchable text.

- Convert web pages to Adobe PDF from Acrobat and directly from a web browser.

 This lesson will take approximately 60 minutes to complete. Copy the Lesson02 folder onto your hard drive if you haven't already done so.

You can easily create PDF files from existing files, such as Microsoft Word documents, web pages, scanned documents, and images.

About creating Adobe PDF files

▶ **Tip:** If you have a Document Cloud subscription, you can convert Microsoft Office and image files to PDF using the Acrobat DC mobile app. To learn more, see "Going mobile" on page 6.

You can convert a variety of file formats to Adobe PDF, preserving all the fonts, formatting, graphics, and color of the source file, regardless of the application and platform used to create it. You can create PDF files from images, document files, websites, scanned paper documents, and clipboard content.

If the document you want to convert to PDF is open in its authoring application (for example, a spreadsheet is open in Excel), you can usually convert the file to PDF without opening Acrobat. But if Acrobat is already open, you don't have to open the authoring application to convert a file to PDF.

When you create a PDF, consider file size and quality (image resolution, for example). When such factors are critical, use a method that allows you to control conversion options. Dragging and dropping files on the Acrobat icon to create PDF files is fast and easy, but if you want more control over the process, use another method, such as using the Create PDF tool in Acrobat or the Print command in the authoring application. After you specify conversion settings, the settings apply across PDFMaker and Acrobat until you change them.

● **Note:** When you're creating a PDF from within Acrobat, you must have the application that created the original file installed on your system.

Lesson 6, "Using Acrobat with Microsoft Office Files (Windows)," describes how to create Adobe PDF files directly from a variety of Microsoft Office files using PDFMaker in Windows. Lesson 7, "Combining Files," covers the conversion of multiple file types as you combine files into a single PDF document. In Lesson 12, "Using Acrobat in Professional Printing," you'll learn how to create press-quality PDF files.

If the security settings applied to an Adobe PDF file allow it, you can also reuse the content of the document. You can extract content for use in another authoring application, such as Microsoft Word, or you can reflow the content for use with handheld devices or screen readers. The success with which content can be repurposed or reused depends very much on the structural information contained in the PDF file. The more structural information a PDF document contains, the more opportunities you have for successfully reusing the content, and the more reliably a document can be used with screen readers. (For more information, see Lesson 3, "Reading and Working with PDF Files.")

Using the Create PDF tool

You can use the Create PDF tool in Acrobat to convert a variety of file types, including both image and non-image files, to Adobe PDF. You'll convert a single TIFF image to an Adobe PDF file.

1 Start Acrobat, if it's not already open.

2 Click Tools to open the Tools Center.

3 Click the Create PDF tool.

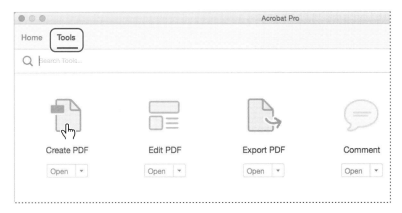

Acrobat displays a list of options for creating a PDF file. Using the Create PDF tool, you can create a PDF document from one or multiple files, a screenshot, a scanned image, a web site, clipboard contents, or a blank page. All your options are easily accessible here. Single File is selected by default.

4 With Single File selected, click Select A File.

5 In the Open dialog box, navigate to the Lesson02 folder on your hard drive, and select the GC_VendAgree.tif file. Then, click Open.

A thumbnail image of the selected file appears, with the filename beneath it.

● **Note:** If the
Advanced Settings
option is dimmed,
there are no additional
settings available for
that file type.

6 Click Advanced Settings.

The settings options vary depending on the file type you've selected. For a TIFF image, the Adobe PDF Settings dialog box includes options for scan optimization, image compression, and color management.

You can also review and edit the settings used to convert your files to PDF in the Convert To PDF panel of the Preferences dialog box.

7 Click Cancel to leave the settings unchanged for this document.

8 Click Create.

Acrobat converts the TIFF file to Adobe PDF and opens the PDF file automatically.

9 Click the Fit One Full Page button (▣) on the Page Controls toolbar so that you can see the entire agreement.

Notice that the handwritten note that the signer of the agreement has added is preserved in the Adobe PDF file.

10 Choose File > Save As, name the file **GC_VendAgree.pdf**, and save it in the Lesson02 folder. Then choose File > Close to close the PDF file.

Creating Adobe PDFs from Microsoft Office files (Mac OS)

In Acrobat DC, you convert Microsoft Office files in Mac OS to Adobe PDF just as you would convert any other file. You can use the Print command in Microsoft Office or the Create PDF tool in Acrobat. Or you can drag the file onto the Acrobat icon on your desktop. Acrobat DC does not offer a version of PDFMaker for the Mac OS version of Microsoft Office. However, if you're using Microsoft Word 2011 for Mac OS, you can create a PDF file by choosing File > Save As Adobe PDF.

For more information, see the relevant topics in this lesson and "Creating PDFs" in Adobe Acrobat DC Help.

Dragging and dropping files

You can also create Adobe PDF files from many documents simply by dragging the file onto the Acrobat icon or into the document pane in Acrobat (Windows). Acrobat uses the conversion settings you specified the last time you converted a file.

Experiment with dragging the RoadieDog.jpg, Pumpkin.jpg, LoyalFan.jpg, and Tulips.jpg files from the Lesson02 folder into the Acrobat document pane (Windows), onto the Acrobat icon on your desktop, or onto the Acrobat icon in the Dock (Mac OS). Close any open PDF files when you are finished. You can save the newly created PDF files or close them without saving.

Converting different types of files

You can use the Multiple Files option in the Create PDF tool to easily convert different types of files to Adobe PDF and combine them into one PDF file. If you're using Acrobat Pro, you can also assemble multiple documents into a PDF Portfolio. You'll learn more about combining files and creating PDF Portfolios in Lesson 7, "Combining Files."

Now, you'll convert a file to Adobe PDF and combine it with several other PDF files.

Assembling the files

First, you'll select the files you want to combine, and specify which pages to include. You'll combine a JPEG image file with several PDF files. You'll include only a single page from one of the PDF documents.

1 In Acrobat, click Tools, and then click the Create PDF tool.

2 Select Multiple Files, and then select Combine Files, and click Next.

Acrobat opens the Combine Files dialog box so that you can assemble your documents.

3 Click the Add Files button in the Combine Files dialog box, and choose Add Files from the menu.

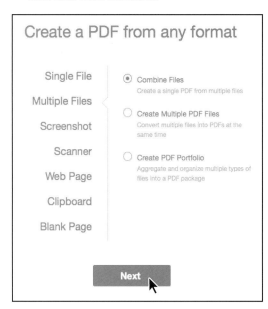
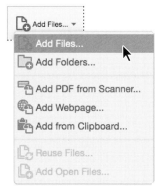

Now you'll select the files that you want to convert and combine. The types of files that you can convert will vary depending on whether you are working in Windows or Mac OS.

4 In the Add Files dialog box, navigate to the MultipleFiles folder in the Lesson02 folder. Make sure that All Supported Formats is selected in the Show menu.

5 Select the Ad.pdf file. Then Shift-click the Data.pdf file to select the bottle.jpg and Data.pdf files, too.

6 Click Open (Windows) or Add Files (Mac OS).

You can add files in any order, because you can rearrange them in the Combine Files window. You can also use the Remove button to remove any unwanted files.

7 Drag the thumbnail of the bottle.jpg file to the right of the Data.pdf file.

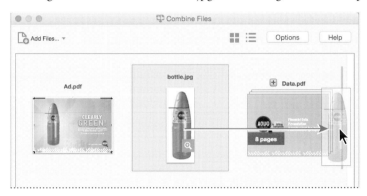

You can convert all pages in a file, or you can select a specific page or range of pages to convert.

8 Click the plus button (+) above the Data.pdf file to see thumbnails of its pages.

9 Select the first page, and click the Remove Selected Items button (🗑) at the bottom of the dialog box.

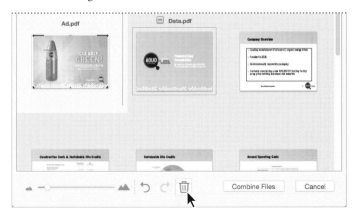

10 Remove all but the second and seventh pages of the Data.pdf file, so that you're left with four thumbnails: Ad.pdf, Data.pdf pages 2 and 7, and bottle.jpg.

11 Click Options to specify settings for the PDF file conversion.

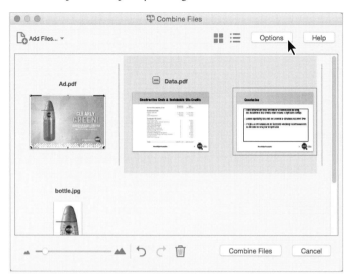

12 In the Options dialog box, make sure the middle icon (Default File Size) is selected for File Size and that Single PDF is selected for File Type. Then click OK.

The Default File Size option produces a PDF file suitable for viewing and printing business documents. The Smaller File Size option optimizes files for web distribution. Use the Larger File Size option to prepare documents for high-quality printing.

13 Click Combine Files.

Acrobat converts any native files into PDF and then consolidates all the selected files into a single file, named Binder1.pdf. The file opens automatically.

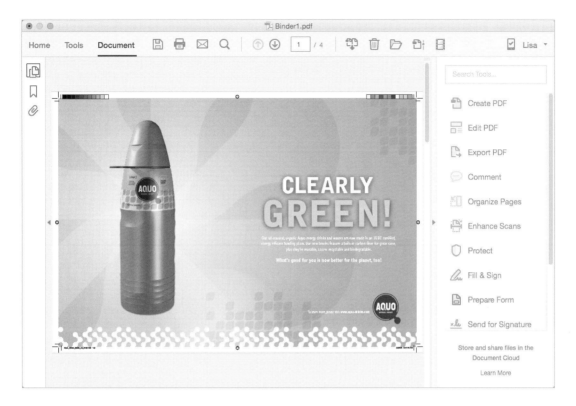

14 Use the Next Page (⊕) and Previous Page (⊕) buttons to page through your consolidated documents.

15 Choose File > Save As. Save the file to the Lesson02 folder, and rename the file **Aquo.pdf**. Click Save.

Without leaving Acrobat, you have converted a JPEG file to Adobe PDF and combined it with other PDF files.

16 Choose File > Close to close the file.

Inserting a blank page

In Acrobat, you can insert blank pages into a PDF file, which makes it easy to create a transition page or a notes page.

1   In Acrobat, open the Aquo.pdf file you created and click the Organize Pages tool in the Tools pane.

2   Choose Insert > Blank Page. In the Insert Pages dialog box, choose After from the Location menu, and select Last Page in the Page area of the dialog box. Then click OK.

The last page is blank, matching the dimensions of the page that preceded it.

3   Choose Edit PDF from the Tools menu on the left side of the Organize Pages toolbar.

The blank page is displayed in the document pane; editing tools are available in the right-hand pane.

4   Click Add Text in the Edit PDF toolbar.

5   Move the pointer over the page; it turns into an I-beam. Click an insertion point at the top of the page.

6   In the Format area of the right-hand pane, change the font (we used Adobe Garamond Pro Bold).

7   Type **Notes**. Use the Format options to change text attributes, including font size and color.

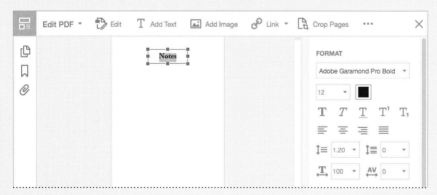

8   Close the file. You can save your changes if you want to.

Using PDFMaker

When you install Adobe Acrobat DC, the installer adds Acrobat PDFMaker buttons or menu commands to supported applications, including Microsoft Office applications (Windows only), Google Chrome (Windows), Mozilla Firefox, Autodesk AutoCAD, and others. PDFMaker options vary from one application to another, but they always give you the ability to quickly create a PDF file from the source application file. Depending on the application, you can also use PDFMaker to add bookmarks, tag the PDF document to make it more accessible, add security features, or include layers.

For specific information about using PDFMaker in Office for Windows, see Lesson 6, "Using Acrobat with Microsoft Office Files (Windows)." To use PDFMaker in Firefox, Chrome, or Internet Explorer, see "Converting web pages to Adobe PDF" later in this lesson.

Using the Print command to create Adobe PDF files

As you saw earlier in this lesson, you can easily create Adobe PDF files using the Create PDF tool in Acrobat. However, you can also create an Adobe PDF file from almost any application by using the application's Print command with the Adobe PDF printer (Windows) or the Save As Adobe PDF option (Mac OS).

Printing to the Adobe PDF printer (Windows)

The Adobe PDF printer isn't a physical printer like one that might sit in your office. Rather, it is a simulated printer that converts your file to Adobe PDF instead of printing it to paper. The printer name is Adobe PDF.

You'll convert a text file to Adobe PDF using the Print command with the Adobe PDF printer. You can use this technique from almost any application, regardless of whether the application has built-in features for creating PDF files. You should be aware, however, that the Adobe PDF printer creates untagged PDF files. (A tagged structure is required for reflowing content to a handheld device and is preferable for producing reliable results with a screen reader.)

Steps may vary depending on the application and whether you are using Windows 7 or Windows 8. These steps assume that you are using Windows 7.

Note: If you simply double-click the file, Windows opens it in Notepad. You can use Notepad for this exercise, but the memo may lose its formatting.

1 From your desktop, navigate to the Lesson02 folder, and select the Memo.txt file.

2 Choose File > Open With > WordPad. Or right-click the file, and choose Open With > WordPad. The text file opens in WordPad, a text editor that comes with Windows.

3 In WordPad in Windows 7, click the menu button, and choose Print.

4 Choose Adobe PDF from the list of printers. You may need to scroll to see it.

To change the settings used to convert the text file to Adobe PDF, click Preferences in the Print dialog box or Properties in the Page Setup dialog box. For more information, see the "Adobe PDF Presets" sidebar later in this lesson.

5 Click Print.

6 Save the file using the default name (Memo.pdf) in the Lesson02 folder, and click Save in the Save PDF File As dialog box.

7 If the PDF file doesn't open automatically, navigate to the Lesson02 folder, and double-click the Memo.pdf file to open it in Acrobat. When you have reviewed the file, close it and quit WordPad.

The Adobe PDF printer is an easy and convenient way to create a PDF file from almost any document. However, if you're working with Microsoft Office files, the Create Adobe PDF buttons or the Acrobat ribbon (which use PDFMaker) let you create tagged documents and include bookmarks and hypertext links.

8 Close any open files.

Printing with the Save As Adobe PDF option (Mac OS)

In Mac OS, use the Save As Adobe PDF option in the PDF menu in the Print dialog box to print from any application.

1 From your desktop, navigate to the Lesson02 folder, and double-click the Memo.txt file.

The text file opens in a text editor such as TextEdit.

2 Choose File > Print. It doesn't matter which printer is selected.

3 Click the PDF button at the bottom of the dialog box, and choose Save As Adobe PDF.

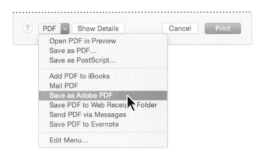

● **Note:** In some applications, such as Adobe InDesign CC, click Printer in the Print dialog box to see the PDF menu.

4 In the Save As Adobe PDF dialog box, choose an Adobe PDF Settings file, and choose Adobe Acrobat from the After PDF Creation menu to open the PDF file in Acrobat.

5 Click Continue.

6 In the Save dialog box, accept the default name of Memo.pdf, and save the file to the Lesson02 folder.

7 Click Save.

The PDF file opens automatically, because you chose Adobe Acrobat from the After PDF Creation menu.

8 Review the file, close it, and quit the text editor application.

You have just converted a simple text document to an Adobe PDF document using the authoring application's Print command.

9 Close any open files.

Adobe PDF presets

A PDF preset is a group of settings that affect the process of creating a PDF file. These settings are designed to balance file size with quality, depending on how the PDF file will be used. Most predefined presets are shared across Adobe Creative Cloud applications, including Adobe InDesign®, Adobe Illustrator®, Adobe Photoshop®, and Acrobat. You can also create and share custom presets to meet your own needs.

For more detailed descriptions of each preset, see Adobe Acrobat DC Help.

- **High Quality Print** creates PDFs for good-quality printing on desktop printers and proofing devices.
- **Oversized Pages** creates PDFs suitable for viewing and printing engineering drawings larger than 200 by 200 inches.
- **PDF/A-1b** standards are used for the long-term preservation (archival) of electronic documents.
- **PDF/X-1a** standards minimize the number of variables in a PDF document to improve reliability. PDF/X-1a files are commonly used for digital ads that will be reproduced on a press.
- **PDF/X-3** files are similar to PDF/X-1a files, but they support color-managed workflows and allow some RGB images.
- **PDF/X-4** has the same color-management ICC color specifications as PDF/X-3, but includes support for live transparency.
- **Press Quality** creates PDF files for high-quality print production (for example, for digital printing or for separations to an imagesetter or platesetter).
- **Smallest File Size** creates PDF files for displaying on the web or an intranet, or for distribution through an email system.
- **Standard** creates PDF files to be printed to desktop printers or digital copiers, published on a CD, or sent to a client as a publishing proof.

Reducing file size

The size of a PDF file can vary dramatically depending on the Adobe PDF settings used to create it. For example, files created using the High Quality Print preset are larger than files created using the Standard or Smallest File Size presets. Regardless of the preset used to create a file, you can often reduce the file size without having to regenerate the PDF file.

You'll reduce the size of the Ad.pdf file.

1   In Acrobat, choose File > Open, navigate to the Lesson02/MultipleFiles folder, and open the Ad.pdf file.

2   Choose File > Save As Other > Reduced Size PDF.

3   Select Acrobat 10.0 And Later for file compatibility, and click OK.

Be sure to choose a version of Acrobat that your intended audience is likely to have.

4   Name the modified file **Ad_Reduce.pdf**. Click Save to complete the process.

It is always a good idea to save a file using a different name so that you don't over-write the unmodified file.

Acrobat automatically optimizes your PDF file, a process that may take a minute or two. Any anomalies are displayed in the Conversion Warnings window. If necessary, click OK to close that window.

5   Minimize the Acrobat window. Use Windows Explorer (Windows) or the Finder (Mac OS) to open the Lesson02/MultipleFiles folder and view the size of the Ad_Reduce.pdf file. The file size is smaller than that of the Ad.pdf file.

You can repeat steps 1–5 using different compatibility settings to see how they affect file size. Note that some settings might actually increase the file size.

6   In Acrobat, choose File > Close to close your file.

Optimizing PDF files (Acrobat Pro only)

Many factors affect file size and file quality, but when you're working with image-intensive files, compression and resampling are important. In Acrobat DC Pro, PDF Optimizer gives you greater control over file size and quality.

To access PDF Optimizer, choose File > Save As Other > Optimized PDF.

In the PDF Optimizer dialog box, you can choose from a variety of file compression methods designed to reduce the file space used by color, grayscale, and mono-chrome images in your document. Which method you choose depends on the kind of images you are compressing. The default Adobe PDF presets use automatic (JPEG) compression for color and grayscale images and CCITT Group 4 compression for monochrome images.

In addition to choosing a compression method, you can resample bitmap images in your file to reduce the file size. A bitmap image consists of digital units called pixels, whose total number determines the file size. When you resample a bitmap image, the information represented by several pixels in the image is combined to make a single larger pixel. This process is also called *downsampling*, because it reduces the number of pixels in the image. (When you downsample or decrease the number of pixels, information is deleted from the image.)

Neither compression nor resampling affects the quality of text or line art.

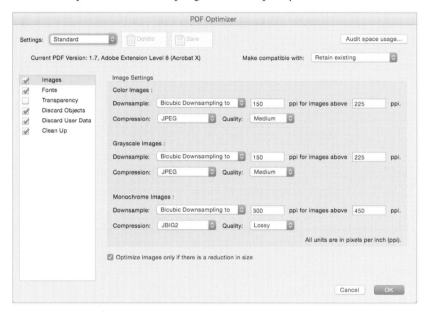

Creating files from the clipboard

You can copy content from any type of file, select Clipboard in the Create PDF tool, and then click Create to create a new PDF file. In Mac OS, you can also select Screenshot in the Create PDF tool to create a PDF file from a window or selection screen capture.

You can also easily add text and graphics that you have copied to the clipboard to an existing PDF. Open the PDF file, select the Organize Pages tool, and then choose Insert > From Clipboard.

Scanning a paper document

You can scan paper documents to PDF from a broad range of scanners, add metadata while scanning, and optimize your scanned PDF. In Windows, you can choose presets for black and white, grayscale, and color documents, as well as color images. These presets optimize the quality of your scanned document. You can also define your own conversion settings.

If you do not have a scanner connected to your system, skip this exercise.

1 Insert any one-page document into your scanner, and do one of the following in Acrobat:

   - **In Windows:** Open the Create PDF tool, select Scanner, and then select a preset for your document. Click Next.

   - **In Mac OS:** Open the Create PDF tool, select Scanner, and click Next. Then select options in the Acrobat Scan dialog box, and click Scan.

The scan occurs automatically.

2 When prompted, click OK to confirm that the scan is complete.

The PDF of the scanned document appears in Acrobat.

3 Choose File > Save, and save the scan in the Lesson02 folder as **Scan.pdf**.

4 In Windows, if you want to see the settings that were used for the conversion, open the Create PDF tool, select Scanner, and click Configure Presets. In this dialog box, you can specify a number of options, including single- or double-sided scanning, paper size, whether to prompt for more pages, file size, application of optical character recognition, and addition of metadata in the Document Properties dialog box. Click Close to exit the dialog box without making any changes.

5 Choose File > Close to close your document.

● **Note:** If Acrobat does not recognize your scanner, refer to your scanner documentation for setup instructions, or contact your scanner manufacturer for troubleshooting help.

Making scanned text editable and searchable

When you convert a file from an application such as Microsoft Word or Adobe InDesign to PDF, the text is fully editable and searchable. However, text in image files, whether scanned documents or files saved in an image format, is not editable and searchable. Using OCR (optical character recognition), Acrobat analyzes the image and replaces portions of it with discrete characters. It also identifies characters it may have analyzed incorrectly.

▶ **Tip:** Acrobat can perform OCR automatically when you scan images. Just make sure Make Searchable is selected in the scanner preset (Windows) or Acrobat Scan dialog box (Mac OS) before you scan.

You'll apply OCR to the PDF document you created from a TIFF image.

1 Choose File > Open, navigate to the Lesson02 folder, and open the GC_VendAgree.pdf file that you saved earlier.

2 Move the pointer over text in the document. You can select areas in the document, but Acrobat does not specifically select any of the text.

3 In the Tools pane, click Enhance Scans, and then choose Recognize Text > In This File.

A toolbar with text recognition options appears below the Enhance Scans toolbar.

4 Click Settings to edit the settings for the conversion.

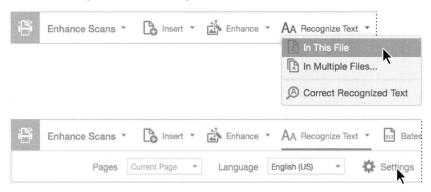

Note: By default, Acrobat converts the document into a searchable image. You can use this setting to convert documents, but the Editable Text And Images option often provides more robust, accurate text conversion.

5 In the Recognize Text dialog box, choose Editable Text And Images from the Output menu. Click OK to close the dialog box.

6 Click Recognize Text in the secondary toolbar.

Acrobat converts the document.

7 Select a word on the page. Acrobat has converted the image to editable, searchable text.

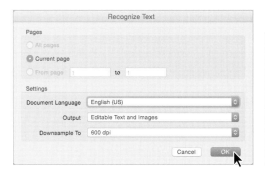

8 Choose Recognize Text > Correct Recognized Text. Acrobat searches the document and identifies any words that may have been converted incorrectly. If it finds any suspect words, you can examine them and correct them as needed. If it doesn't contain any suspects, click OK.

You may also need to use the Edit PDF tool to address issues with spacing.

9 Click Document in the main toolbar to close the Enhance Scans tool.

10 Choose File > Save As. Navigate to the Lesson02 folder, and save the file as **GC_VendAgree_OCR.pdf**. Then close the file.

Converting web pages to Adobe PDF

You can convert or "capture" an entire web page or several levels of a multipage website. From Internet Explorer and Firefox, you can also capture only selected content on a web page. You can define a page layout, set display options for fonts and other visual elements, and create bookmarks for web pages that you convert to Adobe PDF. The HTML file and all associated files—such as JPEG images, cascading style sheets, text files, image maps, and forms—are included in the conversion process, so the resulting PDF behaves much like the original web page.

Because converted web pages are in Adobe PDF, you can easily save them, print them, email them to others, or archive them for your own use.

Converting web pages from within Acrobat

Because web pages are updated on a regular basis, when you visit the web pages described in this lesson, the content of the pages may have changed, and you may have to use links other than those described here. However, you should be able to apply the steps in this lesson to virtually any links on any website. If you are working inside a corporate firewall, for example, you might find it easier to complete this exercise substituting an internal site for the Adobe Press site or the Peachpit site.

Before you can download and convert web pages to Adobe PDF, you must be able to access the web.

Now you'll use the Create PDF tool to convert some web pages.

1 In Acrobat, open the Create PDF tool. (Click Tools to access tools from the Welcome screen.)

2 Select Web Page, and then enter the address of the website you'd like to convert. (We used the Adobe Press website at www.adobepress.com.)

3 Select the Capture Multiple Levels option.

You control the number of converted pages by specifying the levels of site hierarchy you wish to convert, starting from your entered URL. For example, the top level consists of the page corresponding to the specified URL, the second level consists of pages linked from the top-level page, and so on. Consider the number and complexity of pages you may encounter when downloading more than one level of a website at a time. A complex site can take a very long time to download. Therefore, we don't recommend selecting Get Entire Site for most websites. Keep in mind that the time it takes to download pages depends on the speed of your Internet connection.

4 Make sure that the Get option is selected, and that 1 is selected for the number of levels.

5 Select Stay On Same Path to convert only pages that are subordinate to the URL you entered.

6 Select Stay On Same Server to download only pages on the same server as the URL you entered.

7 Click Create.

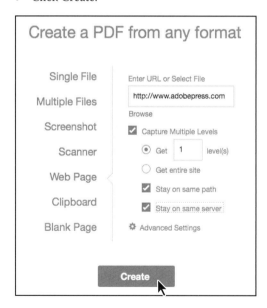

The Download Status dialog box displays the status of the download in progress. When downloading and conversion are complete, the converted website appears in the Acrobat document window, with bookmarks in the Bookmarks panel.

In Windows, if you're downloading more than one level of pages, the Download Status dialog box moves to the background after the first level is downloaded.

If Acrobat cannot download any linked material, it returns an error message. Click OK to clear any error message.

8 Expand the navigation pane, and then click the Bookmarks button to see the bookmarks Acrobat created for the page.

● **Note:** The Adobe Press website changes its content frequently, so your PDF probably won't match ours.

9 Click the Fit One Full Page button (⊞) on the Page Controls toolbar to fit the view of the converted web page to your screen.

10 Use the Next Page (⊙) and Previous Page (⊙) buttons to move through the pages.

The converted website is navigable and editable just like any other PDF document. Acrobat formats the pages to reflect your page-layout conversion settings as well as the look of the original website.

11 Choose File > Save As, name the file **Web.pdf**, and save it in the Lesson02 folder.

Downloading and converting linked pages

When you click a web link in the Adobe PDF version of the web page that links to an unconverted page, you can download and convert that page to PDF, attaching it to the PDF document you created.

1 Navigate through the converted website until you find a web link to a page that wasn't included in your original conversion. We used the title of an article. (The pointer changes to a pointing finger when positioned over a web link, and a tool tip displays the URL of the link.)

2 Right-click (Windows) or Control-click (Mac OS) the link, and choose Append To Document from the context menu.

 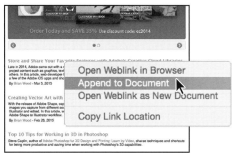

The Download Status dialog box appears again. When the download and conversion are complete, Acrobat displays the linked page, and adds a bookmark for the page to the Bookmarks list.

3 Choose File > Save As, rename the file **Web1.pdf**, and save it in the Lesson02 folder.

4 When you're finished looking at your converted web pages, close the PDF file.

Now you'll convert web pages directly from a browser.

Converting web pages in a web browser

If you've ever had the frustrating experience of printing a web page from your browser only to discover portions of the page missing, you'll appreciate the Acrobat feature that lets you create and print an Adobe PDF version of the web page without ever leaving your browser. You can use PDFMaker in Internet Explorer (Windows), Chrome (Windows), or Firefox (Windows or Mac OS) to convert the currently displayed web page to an Adobe PDF file. When you print a converted web page from Acrobat, the page is reformatted to a standard page size, and logical page breaks are added.

First you'll explore the preferences used to create Adobe PDF pages from your web pages, and then you'll convert a page.

1   Open Firefox, Chrome, or Internet Explorer, and navigate to a favorite web page. We opened the Peachpit Press home page at www.peachpit.com.

2   Click the arrow next to the PDF button (🔳) in Internet Explorer or Firefox; click the PDF button in Chrome. Then choose Preferences from the menu. You can create bookmarks, include headers and footers, add tags, and change page layout features such as orientation.

● **Note:** In Firefox for Mac OS, preferences open in Acrobat.

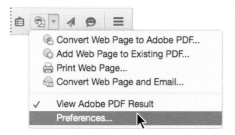

If you don't see the PDF button in Internet Explorer, click the Tools icon, choose Manage Add-ons, and then make sure the Adobe Acrobat Create PDF Toolbar is enabled. In Firefox, choose Tools > Add-ons, and make sure the Adobe Acrobat DC - Create PDF 15 extension is enabled; you may also need to activate the Adobe Acrobat NPAPI plug-in. In Chrome, click the menu button, choose Tools > Extensions, and make sure the Adobe Acrobat - Create PDF extension is enabled.

● **Note:** PDFMaker add-ons are installed with Acrobat. If you install a browser application after installing Acrobat, reinstall Acrobat to install the add-on.

3   Click Cancel to exit the dialog box without making any changes.

Now you'll convert the web page to Adobe PDF.

4   Click the PDF button. Or, click the arrow next to it to display the PDF menu, and then choose Convert Web Page To Adobe PDF.

5   In the Convert Web Page To Adobe PDF dialog box, navigate to the Lesson02 folder. Enter a filename (we used **PeachpitHome.pdf**). Then click Save.

The default filename used by Acrobat is the text used in the HTML tag <TITLE>. Any invalid characters in the web page filename are converted to an underscore when the file is downloaded and saved.

The first level of the website is converted to PDF; the file opens in Acrobat.

6   When you are finished, close the browser, any open PDF files, and Acrobat.

Review questions

1 Name three ways to create a PDF file.

2 How do you print to PDF from an application in Windows?

3 How to you print to PDF from an application in Mac OS?

4 How can you convert an image file to searchable text?

Review answers

1 You can use the Create PDF tool to create a PDF file from almost any format, from a scanned document, from a web page, or from clipboard data. You can use PDFMaker to create a PDF file from within a supporting application, such as Microsoft Office for Windows. You can use the Print dialog box to create a PDF from almost any application.

2 To print to PDF from an application in Windows, select the Adobe PDF printer in the Print dialog box, specify your settings, and click Print.

3 To print to PDF from an application in Mac OS, click the Create PDF button in the Print dialog box, and then choose Save As Adobe PDF. Specify your settings, and click Save.

4 To convert an image file to searchable text, open the Enhance Scans tool, and then choose Recognize Text > In this File. Then click Recognize Text.

3 READING AND WORKING WITH PDF FILES

Lesson overview

In this lesson, you'll do the following:

- Navigate an Adobe PDF document using tools and bookmarks.

- Change how a PDF document scrolls and displays in the document window.

- Search a PDF document for a word or phrase.

- Fill out a PDF form.

- Print all or a portion of a PDF document.

- Explore the accessibility features that make it easier for users with vision and motor impairments to use Acrobat.

- Add tags and Alt text to a PDF document.

- Share a document with others electronically.

 This lesson will take approximately 60 minutes to complete. Copy the Lesson03 folder onto your hard drive if you haven't already done so.

Get the most out of the PDF documents you create
and read using navigational aids, accessibility features,
search tools, and more.

About the onscreen display

▶ **Tip:** To see the printed size of your page, move your pointer into the lower left area of the document pane.

Move the cursor over the bottom of the screen to see the Page Controls toolbar. The magnification shown in the toolbar does not refer to the printed size of the page, but rather to how the page is displayed onscreen. At 100% view, each pixel in the page is represented by one screen pixel on your monitor.

How big the page appears onscreen depends on your monitor size and resolution setting. For example, when you increase the resolution of your monitor, you increase the number of screen pixels within the same monitor area. This results in smaller screen pixels and a smaller displayed page, since the number of pixels in the page itself stays constant.

Reading PDF documents

Acrobat provides a variety of ways for you to move through and adjust the onscreen magnification of a PDF document. For example, you can scroll through the document using the scroll bar at the right side of the window, or you can turn pages as in a traditional book using the Next Page and Previous Page buttons in the main toolbar. You can also jump to a specific page.

Browsing the document

You can move to different pages in a document using a variety of navigation methods.

1 In Acrobat, choose File > Open, navigate to the Lesson03 folder, and select the Pluralist.pdf file. Click Open.

2 Choose View > Zoom > Fit Width to resize your page to fit the width of your screen.

3 Select the Hand tool (🖐) from the Page Controls toolbar, and then position your pointer over the document. Hold down the mouse button. Notice that the pointer changes to a closed hand when you hold down the mouse button.

4 Drag the closed hand up and down in the window to move the page on the screen. This is similar to moving a piece of paper around on a desktop.

5   Press Enter or Return to display the next part of the page. You can press Enter or Return repeatedly to view the document from start to finish in screen-sized sections.

6   Choose View > Zoom > Zoom To Page Level, or click the Fit One Full Page button (⊞) in the Page Controls toolbar. Click the Previous Page button (⬆) in the main toolbar as many times as necessary to return to page 1.

7   Click once in an empty portion of the scroll bar. Or, in Windows, you can also position the pointer over the down arrow in the scroll bar and click.

The document scrolls automatically to display all of page 2. In the next few steps, you'll control how Acrobat scrolls and displays PDF pages.

You can also access the Actual Size, Zoom To Page Level, Fit Width, and Fit Visible commands by clicking the arrow to the right of the magnification pop-up menu in the Page Controls toolbar.

8   Click the Scrolling Mode button (⬚) on the Page Controls toolbar, and then use the scroll bar to scroll to page 3 of 6.

The Scrolling Mode option displays pages end to end, like frames in a filmstrip.

9 Choose View > Page Navigation > First Page to go back to the beginning of the document.

10 Click the Fit One Full Page button (⊞) in the Page Controls toolbar to return to the original page layout.

You can use the page number box in the main toolbar to move directly to a specific page.

11 Type **4** to replace the current page number, and press Enter or Return.

Acrobat displays page 4.

The scroll bar also lets you navigate to a specific page.

12 Begin dragging the scroll box upward in the scroll bar. As you scroll, a page preview box shows you the current page number. When you see page 2 of 6, release the mouse.

The second page is displayed.

Changing the page view magnification

You can change the magnification of the page view using controls in the Page Controls toolbar and commands in the View menu.

1 Choose View > Zoom > Fit Width, or click the Scrolling Mode button in the Page Controls toolbar. A new magnification appears in the Page Controls toolbar.

2 Click the Next Page button (⊙) to move to page 3. Notice that the magnification remains the same.

3 Choose View > Zoom > Actual Size to return the page to a 100% view.

4 In the Page Controls toolbar, click the arrow to the right of the magnification text box to display the preset magnification options. Choose 200%.

You can also type in a specific value for the magnification in the text box.

5 Click the arrow to the right of the magnification box, and choose Actual Size to display the page at 100% again.

Next, you'll use the Zoom In button to magnify the view.

6   Select the page number, type **6**, and press Enter or Return to go to page 6.

7   In the Page Controls toolbar, click the Zoom In button (⊕) once.

8   Click the Zoom In button again to further increase the magnification.

Each click on a Zoom button increases or decreases the magnification by a set amount.

9   Click the Zoom Out button (⊖) twice to return the view to 100%.

Now you'll use the Marquee Zoom tool to magnify the image. The Marquee Zoom tool is hidden by default, so you'll add it to the main toolbar.

10 Choose View > Show/Hide > Toolbar Items > Show Select & Zoom Tools > Marquee Zoom to display the Marquee Zoom tool in the main toolbar.

11 Select the Marquee Zoom tool (⌕). Position the pointer near the upper left corner of the image that includes the letter "O," and drag to the lower right corner.

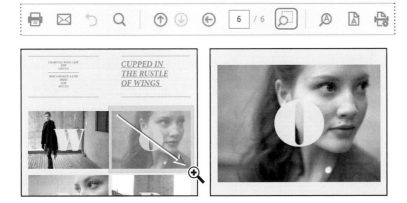

The view zooms in on the area you enclosed.

12 Choose View > Zoom > Zoom To Page Level.

Using the Dynamic Zoom tool

The Dynamic Zoom tool lets you zoom in or out by dragging the mouse up or down.

1   Choose View > Show/Hide > Toolbar Items > Show Select & Zoom Tools > Dynamic Zoom to add the Dynamic Zoom button to the main toolbar.

2   Select the Dynamic Zoom tool (⌕).

▶ **Tip:** You can show or hide other tools in the main toolbar by choosing View > Show/Hide > Toolbar Items, selecting a category, and then selecting the tool you want to display or hide.

3 Click in the document pane. Drag upward to zoom in, and drag down to zoom out.

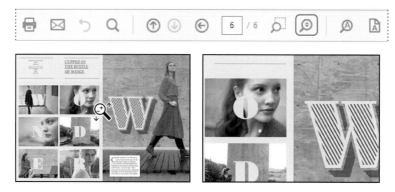

4 When you're finished, select the Hand tool to deselect the Dynamic Zoom tool, and then click the Fit One Full Page button (⊞) in the Page Controls toolbar.

Following links

One benefit of working with electronic documents is that you can convert traditional cross-references into links, which let users jump directly to the referenced section or file. For example, you can make each item in a table of contents a link that jumps to its corresponding area in the document. You can also use links to add interactivity to traditional book elements such as glossaries and indexes.

First you'll add some navigational tools to the main toolbar.

1 Choose View > Show/Hide > Toolbar Items > Show Page Navigation Tools > Show All Page Navigation Tools.

Now you'll use an existing link to move to a specific area in the document.

2 Click the First Page button (⊜) in the main toolbar to return to the first page, and then click the Next Page button (⊕) to move to page 2.

3   Move the pointer over the word "Beauty." The Hand tool changes to a pointing finger, indicating the presence of a link. Click to follow the link.

This link sends you to page 3.

4   Click the Previous View button (⊙) to return to your previous view of page 2.

You can click the Previous View button at any time to retrace your viewing path through a document. The Next View button reverses the action of your last Previous View.

5   To restore the default toolbar configuration, choose View > Show/Hide > Toolbar Items > Reset Toolbars.

Searching PDF documents

You can quickly search for a word or phrase in a PDF document. For example, if you wanted to find occurrences of the word *blouse* in this document, you can use either the Find feature or the Search feature to locate that information. The Find feature locates a word or phrase in the active document. The Search feature locates a word or phrase in one document, across a selection of documents, or in a PDF Portfolio. Both features search text, layers, form fields, and digital signatures.

First you'll use the Find command to find specific text in the open document.

1   Choose Edit > Find. In the text box in the toolbar that appears in the upper right corner of the application window, type **blouse**.

To see the options available with the Find feature, click the arrow on the right side of the text box. You can refine your search, looking for whole words only or specifying uppercase or lowercase letters, and you can also include bookmarks and comments in the search. A check mark next to an option indicates that it is enabled (on).

2 Press Enter or Return to start the Find operation.

The first occurrence of *blouse* is highlighted on page 3 of the document.

3 Click the Next button in the Find panel to find the next occurrence of the word. Acrobat reports that it found no more matches. Click OK to close the dialog box, and then close the Find panel.

Next, you'll perform a more sophisticated search of the document using the Search feature. In this exercise, you'll search only one document, but you can use the Search feature to search all documents in a folder as well as all documents in a PDF Portfolio. You can even search non-PDF files in a PDF Portfolio.

4 Choose Edit > Advanced Search.

5 To search only the open document, select In The Current Document.

In this search, you'll find references to sleeves or dresses.

6 In the Search text box, enter **dress sleeve**.

7 Click the Show More Options link at the bottom of the Search pane.

8 From the Return Results Containing pop-up menu, choose Match Any Of The Words. This ensures that the search will return all results for "dress" or "sleeve," including words that contain additional letters, such as "address."

9 Click Search.

▶ **Tip:** You can also save your search results in Acrobat DC: Click the Save icon next to the New Search button in the Search pane, and then choose either Save Results To PDF or Save Results To CSV.

The search results are displayed in the Search pane.

10 Click any search result to go to the page that contains that information.

You can check any of the other search results in the Search pane by clicking them.

11 When you're finished, close the Search pane.

In addition to text in the document, the Search feature searches object data and image metadata. When you search multiple PDF documents, Acrobat also looks at the document properties and XMP metadata. If any of your PDF documents have attachments, you can also include those attachments in the search. If you include a PDF index in your search, Acrobat searches indexed structure tags. To search an encrypted document, you must first open the document.

Printing PDF documents

Many of the options in the Acrobat Print dialog box are similar to those you'd find in the Print dialog boxes of other popular applications. For example, you can select a printer and set up parameters such as paper size and orientation. However, Acrobat also gives you the flexibility to print only the current view (that is, what is displayed on the screen at that moment), a selection, a specific page, selected pages, or a range of pages within the PDF file.

You'll instruct Acrobat to print pages you select in the Page Thumbnails panel, a particular view, and discontiguous pages.

1 In the Pluralist.pdf document, click the Page Thumbnails button in the navigation pane. Then click three thumbnails to select the pages you want to print. You can Ctrl-click (Windows) or Command-click (Mac OS) page thumbnails to select contiguous or discontiguous pages.

► **Tip:** In Windows, you can also access the Print dialog box by choosing Print from the context menu.

2 Choose File > Print. Select the name of the printer you want to print to. Because you selected pages in the Page Thumbnails panel, the Selected Pages option is selected automatically in the Print dialog box.

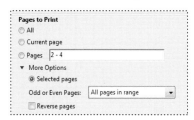

3 Click OK or Print to print your selected pages. Click Cancel if you don't want to print.

If you need help troubleshooting a printing issue, click the Help link in the upper right corner of the Print dialog box to go to the Adobe website for the latest printing tips and information.

4 After the pages print (or the Print dialog box closes, if you opted not to print), click an empty area of the Page Thumbnails panel to deselect all thumbnails, and then close the Page Thumbnails panel.

5 Go to page 5 of the document.

6 Zoom in to 200%, and then use the Hand tool to shift the page so that you see only the model and part of the word "play."

7   Choose File > Print, and select the name of the printer you want to print to.

8   In the Pages To Print area, click More Options. Then select Current View. The preview changes to represent what is currently visible in the document pane.

If you print with Current View selected, Acrobat prints only the contents of the document pane. However, you'll select pages to print instead.

9   In the Pages To Print area, select Pages.

10 In the Pages text box, type **1, 3-4, 6**. If you click OK or Print now, Acrobat will print pages 1, 3, 4, and 6. You can enter any set of discontiguous pages or ranges of pages, using commas, in this text box.

11 If you want to print the pages you've selected, click OK. If you don't want to print, click Cancel.

12 Choose File > Close to close the Pluralist.pdf document.

For information on printing comments, see Lesson 9, "Using Acrobat in a Review Cycle."

If your PDF file contains odd-sized pages, you can use the Size options in the Page Sizing & Handling area of the Print dialog box to reduce, enlarge, or divide pages. The Fit option scales each page to fit the printer page size; pages in the PDF file are magnified or reduced as necessary. The Poster options let you tile oversize pages, printing portions of them on several sheets of paper that can be assembled to reproduce the oversize image. In Windows, you can also specify that the paper source be determined by the document's page size.

Printing booklets

If your printer supports duplex printing, you can print a 2-up, saddle-stitched booklet from Acrobat. Booklets comprise multiple pages that are arranged so that they can be folded to present the correct page order. In a 2-up, saddle-stitched booklet, two side-by-side pages, printed on both sides, are folded once and fastened along the fold. The first and last pages print on the same sheet, the second and next-to-last pages print on the same sheet, and so on. When you collate, fold, and staple the double-sided pages, you create a single book with correct pagination.

To print a booklet from Acrobat:

1 Choose File > Print, and select your printer.

2 In the Pages To Print area, specify which pages to print.

3 In the Page Sizing & Handling area of the Print dialog box, click Booklet.

4 Choose additional page-handling options. You can auto-rotate pages, specify the first and last sheet to print, and select the binding edge. The Preview image changes as you specify options. For information about the options, see "Printing booklets" in Adobe Acrobat DC Help.

Filling out PDF forms

▶ **Tip:** You can fill out PDF forms on a tablet or phone using the Acrobat DC mobile app. For more information, see "Going mobile" on page 6.

PDF forms can be interactive or noninteractive. Interactive PDF forms (also called *fillable forms*) have built-in form fields and behave in much the same way as most forms that you encounter on the web or that are sent to you electronically. You enter data using the Selection tool or Hand tool in Acrobat or Acrobat Reader.

Noninteractive PDF forms (flat forms) are pages that have been scanned to create a facsimile of a form. These pages do not contain actual form fields; they contain only the images of form fields. Traditionally you would print out these forms, fill them out by hand or using a typewriter, and then mail or fax the hard copy. With Acrobat, you can fill out these noninteractive or flat forms online using the Add Text tool.

For information on creating and managing interactive forms, see Lesson 10, "Working with Forms in Acrobat."

You'll fill out fields in an interactive form, and then add information where there is no field using the Add Text tool.

1 Choose File > Open, and navigate to the Lesson03 folder. Select the Registration.pdf file, and click Open.

When it opens the document, Acrobat highlights the form fields.

2 Click in the Address field. Enter an address. The text appears in the font and type size chosen by the form creator.

3 Choose a state (there are four listed) from the State pop-up menu.

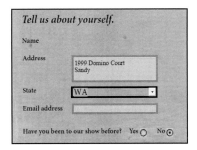

Some fields, such as Address and Email Address, require you to type in text, while check boxes and radio buttons require you only to click to select them. The Email My Reply button performs an action when you click it.

The person who created this form forgot to create an interactive field for the name. You'll add text without requiring a field.

4 In the Tools pane, click the Edit PDF tool to open it. Then click Add Text in the Edit PDF toolbar.

5 Click next to the word *Name*. The pointer is an I-beam.

6 Type your name.

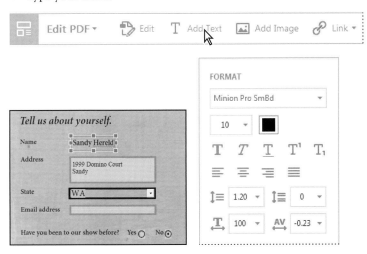

You can use the Add Text tool to add text to any PDF file, unless security applied to the document prohibits it. You can customize the text formatting using options in the Format area of the right-hand pane.

7 Select the Hand tool in the Page Controls toolbar, and select Yes for the last question on the form. Then select No. Only one radio button can be selected at a time, so if you select one, the other is deselected.

8 Click the X in the Edit PDF toolbar to close the tool.

9 Choose File > Save As, and save a copy of the form in the Lesson03 folder, using the filename **Registration_complete.pdf**.

You can open the saved file if you wish to verify that all your data was saved.

10 Choose File > Close to close the form.

About flexibility, accessibility, and structure

The accessibility and flexibility of your Adobe PDF files determine how easily vision- and motion-impaired users and users of handheld devices can access, reflow, and—if you allow it—reuse the content of your files. You control the accessibility and flexibility of your Adobe PDF files through the amount of structure you build into the source file and the method you use to create the Adobe PDF file.

By making your PDF documents more accessible to users, you can broaden your readership and better meet government standards for accessibility. Accessibility in Acrobat falls into two categories:

• Accessibility features that help authors create accessible documents from new or existing PDF documents. These features include simple methods for checking accessibility and adding tags to PDF documents. With Acrobat Pro, you can also correct accessibility and reading-order problems in PDF files by editing the PDF file structure.

• Accessibility features that help readers who have motion or vision limitations to navigate and view PDF documents more easily. Many of these features can be adjusted by using a wizard, the Accessibility Setup Assistant.

For Adobe PDF files to be flexible and accessible, they must have structure. Adobe PDF files support three levels of structure—tagged, structured, and unstructured. Tagged PDF files have the most structure. Structured PDF files have some structure, but are not as flexible or accessible as tagged PDF files. Unstructured PDF files have no structure. (As you will see later in this lesson, you can add limited structure to unstructured files.) The more structure a file has, the more efficiently and reliably its content can be reused.

Structure is built into a document when, for example, its creator defines headers and columns, adds navigational aids such as bookmarks, and adds alternate text descriptions for graphics. In many cases, documents are automatically given logical structure and tags when they are converted to Adobe PDF.

When you create PDF documents from Microsoft Office files or from files created in later versions of Adobe FrameMaker®, InDesign, or Adobe PageMaker®, or when you create Adobe PDF files from websites, the resulting PDF files are tagged automatically.

In Acrobat Pro, if your PDF documents don't reflow well, you can correct most problems using the Accessibility panel or the TouchUp Reading Order tool. However, this is not as easy as creating a well-structured document in the first place. For an in-depth guide to creating accessible PDF documents, visit www.adobe.com/accessibility.

Working with accessible documents

If you're working with Acrobat Pro, you'll examine a tagged PDF document. In either Acrobat Standard or Pro, you'll see how easy it is to reflow the document and extract content.

Checking for accessibility (Acrobat Pro only)

It's always a good idea to check the accessibility of any Adobe PDF document before you distribute it to users. The Accessibility Checker panel tells you if your document has the information necessary to make it accessible. At the same time, it checks for protection settings that would prohibit access.

First you'll look at the accessibility and flexibility of a tagged PDF file that was created from a Microsoft Word file.

1   Choose File > Open, navigate to the Lesson03 folder, and double-click the Tag_Wines.pdf file.

2   Choose File > Save As, and save the file as **Tag_Wines1.pdf** in the Lesson03 folder.

3   In the Tools pane, click the Accessibility tool. If the Accessibility tool isn't listed, click Tools in the main toolbar, choose Add Shortcut from the pop-up menu beneath the Accessibility tool, and click the Accessibility tool in the Tools pane.

▶ **Tip:** By default, Acrobat displays only some of the tools in the Tools pane. To select which tools appear in the list, click Tools in the main toolbar, and then choose Add Shortcut or Remove Shortcut beneath each tool.

You'll use the Accessibility tool several times in this lesson, so it's handy to have it in the Tools pane. You can remove a tool from the Tools pane at any time by choosing Remove Shortcut from the menu beneath the tool in the Tools Center.

Accessibility options appear in the right-hand pane.

4   Click Full Check in the right-hand pane.

5   Accept the defaults in the Accessibility Checker Options dialog box, and click Start Checking.

Acrobat quickly checks the document for accessibility issues, and displays the interactive Accessibility Checker panel in the navigation pane. There are some issues with this document.

6   Expand the Document category. It lists three issues. Two of those issues are items that require you to look at the document to determine whether there's a problem (Logical Reading Order and Color Contrast). The third issue is the Title, which failed.

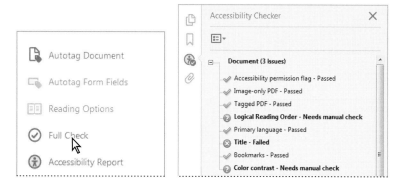

In an accessible document, the document title should be included and set to display automatically in the title bar. You can learn what each item in the Accessibility Checker panel refers to by choosing Explain from the options menu at the top of the panel.

7   Right-click or Control-click the Title item, and choose Fix.

The panel changes to show that the title passed, after Acrobat changed its settings. Had there not been a title already in the document, you'd have been prompted to enter the document title. You can quickly fix most accessibility issues in a document using the interactive Accessibility Checker panel.

8   Close the Accessibility Checker panel and the Accessibility tool.

You can add security to your PDF files and still make them accessible. The encryption offered by Acrobat DC prevents users from copying and pasting text from a PDF file, while still supporting assistive technology.

Reflowing a flexible PDF file (Standard and Pro)

Now you'll take a quick look at how flexible a tagged PDF file is. You'll reflow the PDF file, and then you'll save the contents of the PDF file as accessible text.

First, you'll adjust the size of your document window to mimic the smaller screen of a handheld device.

1   Choose View > Zoom > Actual Size to display the document at 100%.

2   Resize the Acrobat window to about 50% of the full-screen display. In Windows, click the Maximize/Restore Down button if the window is currently maximized; if the window isn't maximized, drag a corner of the application window to reduce it. In Mac OS, resize the document pane by dragging a corner.

Your goal is to resize the Acrobat window so that the ends of the sentences in the document pane are cut off.

3   Choose View > Zoom > Reflow.

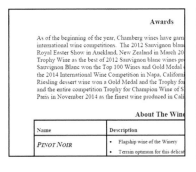

The content of the document is reflowed to accommodate the smaller document screen, and you can now read an entire line of text without using the horizontal scroll bar.

When you reflow text, artifacts such as page numbers and page headers often drop out because they are no longer relevant to the page display. Text is reflowed one page at a time. You cannot save the document in the reflowed state.

Now you'll examine how the display changes when you change the magnification.

4   Choose 400% from the magnification menu in the Page Controls toolbar.

5   Scroll down the page to see how the text reflows. Again, because the text is reflowed, you don't have to use the horizontal scroll bar to move back and forth across the page to read the enlarged text. The text is automatically contained within the document pane.

6 When you've finished viewing the reflowed text, restore the Acrobat document window to its usual size, and close the file.

You can save the contents of a tagged document in a different file format for reuse in another application. For example, if you save this file as accessible text, you'll see that even the contents of the table are saved in an easy-to-use format.

With Acrobat, you can even make some unstructured documents more readily accessible to all types of users. You can add tags to a PDF document using the Add Tags To Document command in any version of Acrobat. However, to correct tagging and order errors, you must be using Acrobat Pro.

Making files flexible and accessible (Acrobat Pro only)

● **Note:** You can add tags and alternate text using tools in the Accessibility panel in Acrobat Standard.

Some tagged Adobe PDF documents may not contain all the information necessary to make their contents fully flexible or accessible. For example, your file may not contain alternate text for figures, language properties for portions of the text that use a different language than the default language for the document, or expansion text for abbreviations. (Designating the appropriate language for different text elements ensures that the correct characters are used when you reuse the document for another purpose, that the word can be pronounced correctly when read out loud, and that the document will be spell-checked with the correct dictionary.)

If you're using Acrobat Pro, you can add alternate text and multiple languages using the Tags panel. (If only one language is required, it is easier to choose the language in the Document Properties dialog box.) You can also add alternate text using the TouchUp Reading Order tool.

Using the Make Accessible action

If you're using Acrobat Pro, you can systematically ensure your PDF document is accessible using the Make Accessible action. You'll use the action to set document properties, set the tab order, add tags, and add alternate text to the document.

The Make Accessible action is one of the default actions in the Action Wizard in Acrobat Pro. You'll learn more about using and creating actions in Lesson 11, "Using Actions."

First, you'll check the accessibility of a page of a user guide. This document was designed to be printed, so no attempt was made to make it accessible.

1 Choose File > Open, and open the AI_UGEx.pdf file in the Lesson03 folder.

2 Click the Accessibility tool in the Tools pane to open it.

3 Click Full Check, and click Start Checking.

The Accessibility Checker panel indicates that the document isn't tagged (in the Document category). You'll let Acrobat tag the document and add other accessibility features for you.

4 Click Tools in the toolbar, and then choose Open from the pop-up menu beneath the Action Wizard tool.

5 Click Make Accessible in the Actions List pane.

The Actions List pane is replaced by the Make Accessible action pane, which lists the steps included in the action. The action automates steps when possible, and guides you through the steps you need to perform to make your document accessible.

6 Verify that the file in the Files To Be Processed box is AI_UGEx.pdf.

7 Click Start.

The first section of the Make Accessible action helps you prepare your document settings for flexibility and accessibility.

8 In the Description dialog box, deselect Leave As Is in the Title area, change the title to **User Guide**, and click OK.

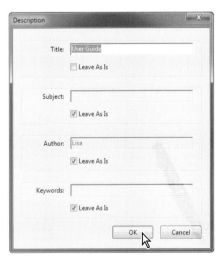

The title in the Description dialog box will appear in the title bar when the document is opened. After you click OK, Acrobat performs the next step automatically, setting the appropriate Open options for the document.

9 Accept the default settings in the Recognize Text - General Settings dialog box, and click OK.

These settings determine how OCR is applied to recognize text for screen readers.

10 When asked whether this document is intended to be a fillable form, click No, Skip This Step.

If this were a form, Acrobat would detect the form fields.

11 Click OK in the Set Reading Language dialog box to accept English as the reading language.

Acrobat automatically performs the next step, adding tags to the document.

12 Click OK when alerted that Acrobat will display any figures with missing alternate text.

Screen readers use alternate text (often called alt text) to describe non-text elements such as images or figures to a visually impaired person. Acrobat examines your document to ensure that every image has alternate text assigned to it, and prompts you to assign text where it's missing.

13 In the Set Alternate Text dialog box, type **Page Tool** as the alt text for the selected image. Then click Save & Close.

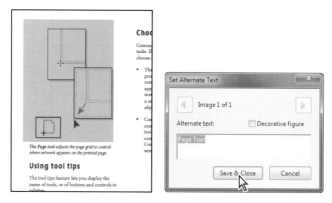

14 Click Start Checking in the Accessibility Checker Options dialog box to confirm that the document is now accessible.

The Accessibility Checker panel now shows only two issues, both items that you would need to confirm manually.

15 Close the Accessibility Checker panel and the Action Wizard tool. Then close the AI_UGEx.pdf document.

About tags

When you add tags to a document, Acrobat adds a logical tree structure to the document that determines the order in which page content is reflowed and read by screen readers and the Read Out Loud feature. If you're using Acrobat Pro, you can let Acrobat add tags automatically using the Make Accessible action. In either Acrobat Pro or Acrobat Standard, you can use the Autotag Document option in the Accessibility tool to assign tags, and then review the resulting Recognition Report to see how successful Acrobat was. On more complex pages—pages that contain irregularly shaped columns, bulleted lists, text that spans columns, and so on—Acrobat may mark areas that require some attention. Use the report to navigate to the problem areas of your PDF document by clicking the links for each error. Then, if you're using Acrobat Pro, click Reading Order in the Accessibility tool to correct the problem.

To see how Acrobat has tagged the document, click the Tags button to open the Tags panel in the navigation pane. (If the Tags button isn't displayed, choose View > Show/Hide > Navigation Panes > Tags.) Click the arrow next to Tags to view the tags.

▶ **Tip:** The Recognition Report is a temporary file and can't be saved. The Full Check feature generates an accessibility report that you can save.

Using Acrobat accessibility features (Standard and Pro)

Many people with vision and motor impairments use computers, and Acrobat provides a number of features that make it easier for them to work with PDF files. Such features include:

- Automatic scrolling
- Keyboard shortcuts
- Support for several screen-reader applications, including the text-to-speech engines built into Windows and Mac OS platforms
- Enhanced onscreen viewing

Using the Accessibility Setup Assistant

Both Acrobat DC and Acrobat Reader include an Accessibility Setup Assistant. In Windows, the Accessibility SetupAssistant launches automatically the first time the software detects a screen reader, screen magnifier, or other assistive technology on your system. In Mac OS, choose Edit > Accessibility Setup Assistant to open it. (You can also launch the Assistant manually at any time by selecting Setup Assistant in the Accessibility tool in Acrobat.) The Accessibility Setup Assistant walks you through setting the options that control how PDF documents appear onscreen. You can also use it to set the option that sends print output to a Braille printer.

A full explanation of the options you can set in the Accessibility Setup Assistant is available in Adobe Acrobat DC Help. The options available depend on the type of assistive technology you have on your system. The first panel of the Accessibility Setup Assistant requires you to identify the type of assistive technology you use:

- Select Set Options For Screen Readers if you use a device that reads text out loud or sends output to a Braille printer.

- Select Set Options For Screen Magnifiers if you use a device that makes text appear larger on the screen.

- Select Set All Accessibility Options if you use a combination of assistive devices.

- Click Use Recommended Settings And Skip Setup to use the settings Adobe recommends for users with limited accessibility. (Note that the preferred settings for users with assistive technology installed are not the same as the default Acrobat settings for users who are not using assistive technology.)

In addition to the options you can set using the Accessibility Setup Assistant, you can select a number of options in the Acrobat or Acrobat Reader preferences that control automatic scrolling, reading-out-loud settings, and reading order. You may want to use some of these options even if you don't have assistive technology on your system. For example, you can set your Multimedia preferences to show available descriptions for video and audio attachments.

If you opened the Accessibility Setup Assistant, click Cancel to exit the dialog box without making any changes.

About automatic scrolling

When you're reading a long document, the automatic scrolling feature saves you keystrokes and mouse actions. You can control the speed of scrolling, scroll backward and forward, and exit automatic scrolling with a single keystroke.

Now you'll test the automatic scroll feature.

1 Choose File > Open, and open the Pluralist.pdf file. If necessary, resize the Acrobat window to fill your desktop.

2 Choose View > Page Display > Automatically Scroll.

3   You can set the rate of scrolling using the number keys on your keyboard. The higher the number, the faster the rate of scrolling. Try pressing 9, and then pressing 1, for example, to change the rate of scrolling. To exit automatic scrolling, press the Esc key.

4   Close the Pluralist.pdf file.

About keyboard shortcuts

For some common commands and tools, the keyboard shortcut is displayed next to the command or tool name. A list of keyboard shortcuts is available in Adobe Acrobat DC Help.

You can also use the keyboard to control Acrobat within a web browser. If the focus is on the web browser, any keyboard shortcuts you use act according to the web browser settings for navigation and selection. Pressing the Tab key shifts the focus from the browser to the Acrobat document and application, so navigation and command keystrokes function normally. Pressing Ctrl+Tab or Command+Tab shifts the focus from the document back to the web browser.

Modifying onscreen elements

You can smooth text, line art, and images to improve onscreen readability, especially with larger text sizes. If you use a laptop or if you have an LCD screen, you can also choose a Smooth Text option to optimize your display quality. Set the options to smooth text in the Page Display preferences.

You can change the color of the background or text displayed on your monitor using the Accessibility Preferences in Acrobat. Color changes affect only the onscreen display, not the printed page or the saved PDF file.

You can increase the text size used in bookmark labels by choosing Text Size > Large from the options menu of the Bookmarks panel.

You may want to experiment with screen-display options and other accessibility controls to find a combination that best suits your needs.

Setting screen reader and reading-out-loud preferences

After you have installed your screen reader or similar application and set it up to work with Acrobat, you can set the screen reader preferences in Acrobat. You set these preferences in the same panel in which you set the Read Out Loud feature preferences that control the volume, pitch, and speed of the speech; the nature of the voice; and the reading order preferences.

Newer systems (both Windows and Mac OS) have built-in text-to-speech engines. Although the Read Out Loud feature can read the text of a PDF file out loud, it is not a screen reader. Not all systems support the Read Out Loud feature.

In this exercise, you'll look at the preferences that affect how Adobe PDF documents are read out loud. Unless you have text-to-speech software on your system, you do not need to set these preferences.

1 Choose File > Open, and open the Tag_Wines.pdf file.

2 If your system has text-to-speech software, choose View > Read Out Loud > Activate Read Out Loud.

3 After you have activated the Read Out Loud feature, choose View > Read Out Loud > Read This Page Only. Acrobat reads the page that is currently displayed. To stop the reading, press Shift+Ctrl+E (Windows) or Shift+Command+E (Mac OS).

You can experiment with the reading options.

4 Choose Edit > Preferences (Windows) or Acrobat > Preferences (Mac OS), and select Reading from the list on the left. Experiment, if you like.

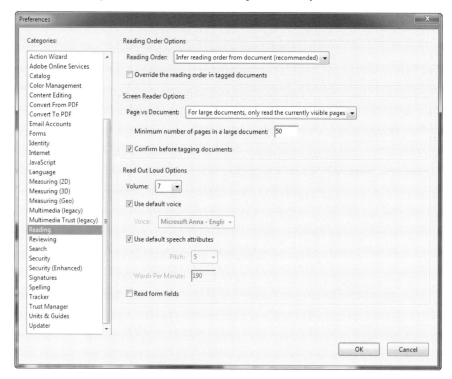

You can control the volume, pitch, speed, and voice used. If you use the default voice, you cannot change the pitch and speed of delivery.

If your system has limited memory, you may wish to reduce the number of pages Acrobat reads before data is delivered page by page. The default value is 50 pages.

5   Click OK in the Preferences dialog box to apply any changes that you make. Or click Cancel to exit the Preferences dialog box without making any changes.

6   To test the settings you changed, choose View > Read Out Loud > Read This Page Only.

7   To stop the reading, press Ctrl+Shift+E (Windows) or Command+Shift+E (Mac OS).

Sharing PDF files

You can share a PDF document with other people in many ways, including posting it on a website, copying it to a flash drive, or sending it as an email attachment. Acrobat makes it easy to distribute a PDF document to others by attaching the document to an email message or using Adobe Send.

Sending email attachments

You can send a PDF file as an attachment to a message you send from an email application on your computer (such as Microsoft Outlook) or from a webmail application such as Gmail or Yahoo Mail.

1   With the Tag_Wines.pdf file open, click the Send Email button (✉) in the main toolbar, and choose Attach To Email.

2   In the Send Email dialog box, select either Default Email Application or Use Webmail. If you select Use Webmail, choose a webmail service from the pop-up menu, and then add the account.

Once you've added a webmail account, it appears in the pop-up list so you can select it directly.

3   Click Continue.

4   If you're using a webmail account, sign in, and grant access to Acrobat if prompted.

Your email application or webmail program opens with a draft message that has the file attached to it. If you're using Gmail, you may need to click Drafts to see the draft message.

5   Enter email addresses, a subject line, and a brief message.

6   Send the message.

Using Adobe Send

Adobe Send uploads a document to Adobe Document Cloud, a secure web service. It sends email to the recipients you specify so that they can read the file online or download it. You need an Adobe ID and a Document Cloud subscription (included with a Creative Cloud subscription) to upload files to Document Cloud.

1 With the Tag_Wines.pdf file open, click the Send Email button (✉) in the Quick Tools toolbar, and choose Send & Track.

2 Select Create Anonymous Link to share the file with anyone who has the link.

If you want to track who has viewed a document you're sharing, select Send Personalized Invitations, and then add email addresses and a message.

3 Click Create Link.

Acrobat copies your document to Document Cloud.

4 Select Email Link or Copy Link.

If you select Email Link, choose an email application or webmail application to use. If you select Copy Link, Acrobat copies the link to the clipboard so you can paste it into an email message, website, or other communication.

5 Click Close, and then close the document.

Review questions

1   Name three methods you can use to navigate to a different page within a document in Acrobat DC.

2   Name two ways to change the view magnification in a PDF file.

3   How can you determine whether a PDF document is accessible when you're working with Acrobat Pro?

4   How can you print pages that are not next to each other (that is, discontiguous pages) from Acrobat?

Review answers

1   You can move to a different page by clicking the Previous Page or Next Page button in the main toolbar; dragging the scroll box in the scroll bar; entering a page number in the page box in the toolbar; or clicking a bookmark, page thumbnail, or link that jumps to a different page.

2   You can change the view magnification by choosing View > Zoom, and then choosing a view; dragging the Marquee Zoom tool; choosing a preset magnification in the Page Controls toolbar; or entering a specific percentage in the magnification text box in the Page Controls toolbar.

3   To determine whether a PDF file is accessible in Acrobat Pro, open the Accessibility tools, and then click Full Check.

4   To print discontiguous pages, either select the page thumbnails, and then choose File > Print, or, in the Print dialog box, select Pages, and then enter the page numbers or ranges you want to print, separated by commas.

4 ENHANCING PDF DOCUMENTS

Lesson overview

In this lesson, you'll do the following:

- Rearrange pages in a PDF document.

- Rotate and delete pages.

- Insert pages into a PDF document.

- Edit links and bookmarks.

- Renumber pages in a PDF document.

- Learn how to insert video and other multimedia files.

- Set document properties and add metadata to a PDF.

 This lesson will take approximately 45 minutes to complete. Copy the Lesson04 folder onto your hard drive if you haven't already done so.

You can modify PDF documents by rearranging, cropping, deleting, or inserting pages; editing text or images; or adding multimedia files. You can also add navigational aids such as bookmarks and links.

Examining the work file

You'll work with conference materials for the fictitious Meridien Conference. The presentation has been designed both for print and for online viewing. Because this online presentation is in the developmental phase, it contains a number of mistakes. You'll use Acrobat to correct the problems in this PDF document.

1   Start Acrobat.

2   Choose File > Open. Navigate to the Lesson04 folder, select Conference Guide.pdf, and click Open. Then choose File > Save As, rename the file **Conference Guide_revised.pdf**, and save it in the Lesson04 folder.

3   Click the small arrow on the left side of the window to open the navigation pane, if it's not already open. Then click the Bookmarks button (▢) in the navigation pane.

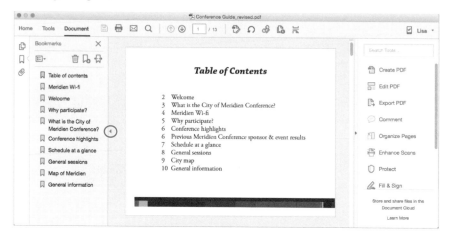

The Bookmarks panel opens, revealing several bookmarks that have already been created. Bookmarks are links to specific points in the document. They can be generated automatically from the table-of-contents entries of documents created by most desktop publishing programs or from formatted headings in applications such as Microsoft Word. You can also create bookmarks in Acrobat. You can specify the appearance of bookmarks and add actions to them.

4   Click anywhere on the Table of Contents page, and then press the Down Arrow key on your keyboard to page through the document.

Notice that the bookmark icon corresponding to the page that you are viewing is highlighted as you move through the pages. (There are a couple of bookmark errors that you'll correct later.)

5   Click the Table of Contents bookmark to return to the first page of the presentation.

6   In the document pane, move the pointer over the items listed in the table of contents. Notice that the hand changes to a pointing finger, indicating that items in the list are links.

7   Click the Meridien Wi-fi entry in the document pane to follow its link. (Be sure to click the entry in the table of contents, not the bookmark in the Bookmarks panel.)

Notice that the page number on the page displayed in the document pane is 2, though the page number in the table of contents showed the page as being page 4. The page is out of order.

8   Choose View > Page Navigation > Previous View to return to the table of contents.

Moving pages with page thumbnails

Page thumbnails offer a convenient way to preview pages. In previous lessons, you used page thumbnails to navigate a document. Now you'll use them to quickly rearrange pages in a document.

1   Click the Page Thumbnails button (⬚) in the navigation pane.

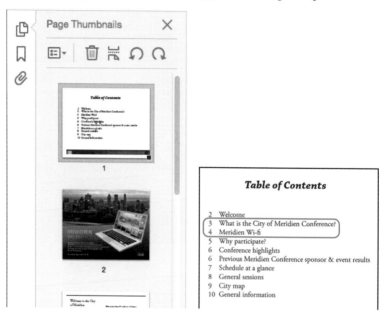

The Meridien Wi-fi page is out of place. According to the table of contents, it should follow the page titled "What is the City of Meridien Conference?"

2   Click the page 2 thumbnail to select it.

3   Drag the selected thumbnail image down until the insertion bar appears between the thumbnails of pages 4 and 5.

4 Release the mouse button to insert the page at its new position.

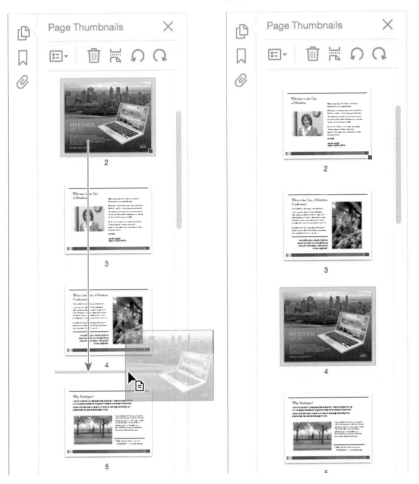

The Meridien Wi-fi page now follows the "What is the City of Meridien Conference?" page and precedes the "Why participate?" page.

5 To check the sequence of pages, choose View > Page Navigation > First Page to go to the first page of the document (if you're not already there), and then use the Next Page button (⊕) to page through the presentation.

6 When you're satisfied that the pages are in the correct order, click the Page Thumbnails button again to close its panel. Then choose File > Save to save your work so far.

Manipulating pages

If you look at the first page of the presentation (page 1 of 13), you'll notice that the first page, the Table of Contents page, is rather plain. To make the presentation more attractive, you'll add a cover page, which you'll then rotate to match the other pages in the presentation.

Inserting a page from another file

You'll start by inserting the cover page.

▶ **Tip:** If you insert a page that is larger than the other pages in a document, you can crop out unnecessary areas of the page. Right-click the page and choose Crop Pages.

1 Open Organize Pages in the Tools pane.

2 Click Insert in the Organize Pages toolbar, and then choose From File.

3 Navigate to the Lesson04 folder, and select Conference Guide Cover.pdf. Click Open or Select.

4 In the Insert Pages dialog box, choose Before from the Location menu, and select First in the Page area. Then click OK. You want to insert this PDF file before any of the pages in your document.

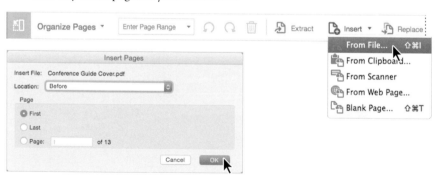

The cover document appears as page 1 in the Conference Guide_revised.pdf document.

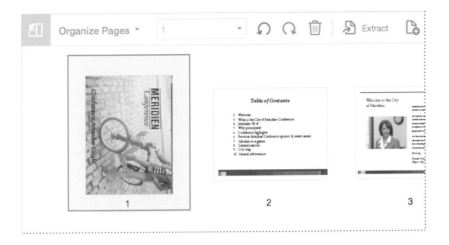

5 Choose File > Save to save your work.

Rotating a page

The cover page is now in the conference document, but it has the wrong orientation. You'll rotate the new page to match the rest of the document.

1 Select the thumbnail for the cover. Two rotation icons and a delete icon appear superimposed on the thumbnail.

2 Click the Rotate Counterclockwise icon.

▶ **Tip:** If you have a Document Cloud subscription, you can rotate and rearrange pages on a tablet or phone using the Acrobat DC mobile app. See "Going mobile" on page 6 to learn more.

Acrobat rotates the page so that it matches the rest of the document. Only the selected page was rotated.

Deleting a page

The last page in the document doesn't quite fit with the others, and the conference committee has decided to distribute it separately. You'll delete it from the document.

1 Select the thumbnail for the last page in the document (page 14).

2 Click the delete icon.

3 Click OK to confirm that you want to delete the page.

The page is deleted from the Conference Guide_revised.pdf file.

4 Close the Organize Pages toolbar to return to the main document view.

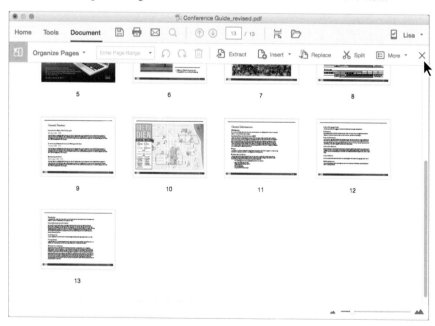

5 Choose File > Save to save your work.

Renumbering pages

You may have noticed that the page numbers on the document pages do not always match the page numbers that appear below the page thumbnails and on the toolbar. Acrobat automatically numbers pages with Arabic numerals, starting with page 1 for the first page in the document, and so on. However, you can change the way Acrobat numbers pages. You'll give the cover page a roman numeral, so that the contents page is page 1.

1   Click the Page Thumbnails button (⬚) in the navigation pane to display the page thumbnails.

2   Click the page 1 thumbnail to go to the cover page.

You'll renumber the first page of the document—the cover page—using lowercase roman numerals.

3   Click the options menu button at the top of the Page Thumbnails panel, and choose Page Labels. The Page Numbering dialog box opens.

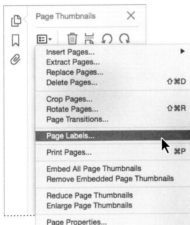

4 For Pages, select From and enter from **1** to **1** of 13. For Numbering, select Begin New Section, choose "i, ii, iii" from the Style menu, and enter **1** in the Start text box. Click OK.

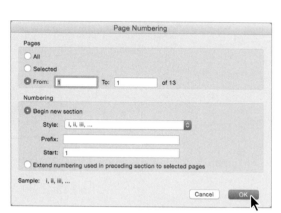
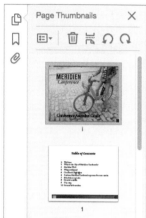

5 Choose View > Page Navigation > Go To Page. Enter **1**, and click OK.

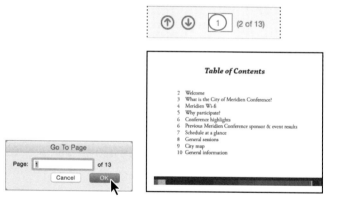

Tip: You can manually add page numbers to the pages of your Adobe PDF document using headers or footers. (Select the Edit PDF tool, and choose Header & Footer > Add.)

Acrobat displays the table of contents page. Because you renumbered the cover page, the number 1 in the page number text box is now assigned to the contents page of the document.

6 Close the Page Thumbnails panel.

7 Choose File > Save to save your changes.

Applying Bates numbering (Acrobat Pro only)

In law offices, Bates numbering is routinely applied to each page of a document that is part of a legal case or process. Using Acrobat DC Pro, you can automatically apply Bates numbering as a header or footer to any document or to documents in a PDF Portfolio. (If the PDF Portfolio contains non-PDF files, Acrobat converts the files to PDF and add Bates numbering.) You can add custom prefixes and suffixes, as well as a date stamp. And you can specify that the numbering is always applied outside the text or image area on the document page.

To apply Bates numbering, click Organize Pages in the Tools pane, and then choose More > Bates Numbering > Add.

In the Bates Numbering dialog box, add the files you want to number, and arrange them in the appropriate order. Click Output Options to specify the location and naming convention for the numbered files. Then use the Add Header And Footer dialog box to define the style and format of the number, which can have 6 to 15 digits, plus prefixes and suffixes.

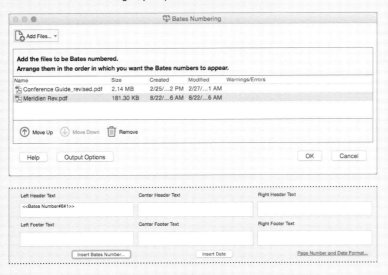

You cannot edit Bates page numbering after you've added it to a document. You can, however, delete Bates numbering and apply a different Bates numbering formula.

For more information on applying Bates numbering and working with other legal features in Acrobat, see Adobe Acrobat DC Pro Help.

Managing links

▶ Tip: To quickly return to your previous view, choose View > Page Navigation > Previous View, or press Ctrl or Command and the Left Arrow key.

Now you'll correct the broken links on the contents page and add a missing link.

1   Go to page 1, the table of contents page, if you're not there already.

2   Click the links for each of the table of contents entries to identify problems.

The link for page 3 and the second link for page 6 go to the wrong pages. There is no link for the last entry. First, you'll correct the links that go to the wrong pages.

3   Click Edit PDF in the Tools pane, and then choose Link > Add Or Edit. Acrobat outlines the links on the page.

4   Double-click the link for page 3, "What is the City of Meridien Conference?"

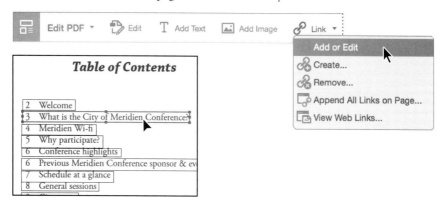

5   In the Link Properties dialog box, click the Actions tab. The action associated with this link is to go to page 3. Click Edit.

6   In the Go To A Page In This Document dialog box, select Use Page Number, and enter **3** in the Page box. Click OK.

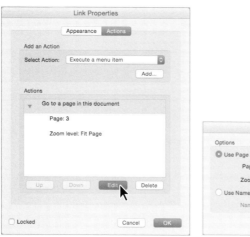
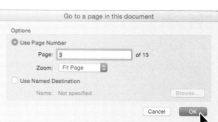

The listed action now goes to page 4. Remember that you renumbered the pages, so page 3 is actually the 4th page in the PDF file.

7 Click OK.

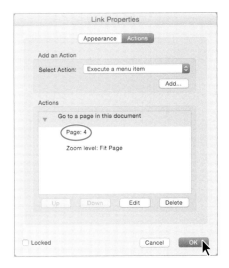

8 Hover over the lower area of the window to view the navigation controls, and select the Selection tool. Then click the link for page 3. It goes to the appropriate page now. Return to the table of contents page.

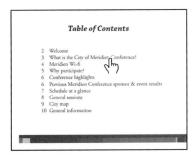 

9 Follow steps 3–7 to make the same change for the link to the previous event results, changing the linked page number to page 6.

Now you'll create a link for the last entry.

10 Go to page 1 (the Table of Contents page), if you're not there already. If links aren't outlined, choose Link > Add Or Edit.

11 Drag a link box around the final contents entry, "10 General information."

12 In the Create Link dialog box, choose Invisible Rectangle for the Link Type, and select Go To A Page View in the Link Action area. Then click Next.

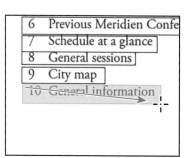 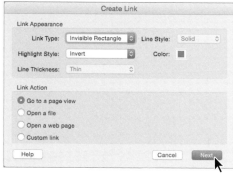

13 Scroll to page 10. When the General Information page is on the screen, click Set Link. Acrobat returns you to the contents page.

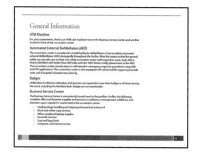 

14 Select the Selection tool, and then click the link you just created to test it.

15 Close the Edit PDF panel.

16 Choose File > Save to save your work.

Working with bookmarks

A bookmark is simply a link represented by text in the Bookmarks panel. While bookmarks that are created automatically by many authoring programs are generally linked to headings in the text or to figure captions, you can also add your own bookmarks in Acrobat to create a custom outline of a document or to open other documents.

Additionally, you can use electronic bookmarks as you would paper bookmarks— to mark a place in a document that you want to highlight or return to later.

Adding a bookmark

First, you'll add a bookmark for the second topic on page 6, the section titled "Previous Meridien Conference sponsor and event results."

1 Go to page 6 in the document, so that you can see the event results.

2 Open the Bookmarks panel, and then click the Conference highlights bookmark. Your new bookmark will be added directly below the selected bookmark.

3 Click the New Bookmark button (🔖) at the top of the Bookmarks panel. A new, untitled bookmark appears.

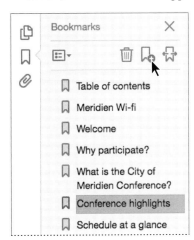 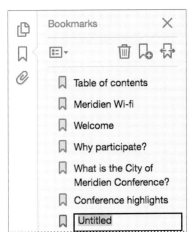

4 In the text box of the new bookmark, type **Previous conference results**. Press Enter or Return to accept the name.

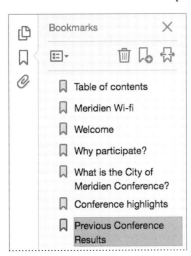 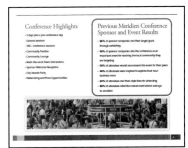

Changing a bookmark destination

A couple of bookmarks link to the wrong pages. You'll change those now.

1   In the Bookmarks panel, click the Why participate? bookmark. The document pane displays the "What is the City of Meridien Conference?" page.

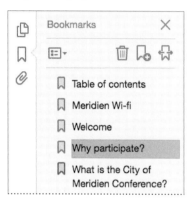

2   Click the Next Page button (⊕) twice to go to page 5 (6 of 13) of the document, which is the page you want the bookmark to link to.

3   From the options menu at the top of the Bookmarks panel, choose Set Bookmark Destination. Click Yes in the confirmation message to update the bookmark destination.

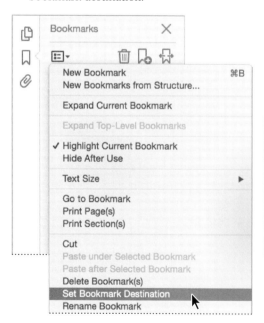

4   Repeat the process to correct the destination of the "What is the City of Meridien Conference?" bookmark, which should be linked to page 3 (4 of 13).

5   Choose File > Save to save the Conference Guide_revised.pdf file.

Naming bookmarks automatically

You can create, name, and automatically link a bookmark by selecting text in the document pane.

1   Navigate to the page you want to link, and set the magnification to the optimal level. The current magnification will be inherited by the bookmark.

2   Drag the I-beam to highlight the text that you want to use as your bookmark.

3   Click the New Bookmark button at the top of the Bookmarks panel. A new bookmark is created in the bookmarks list, and the highlighted text from the document pane is used as the bookmark name. By default, the new bookmark links to the current page view displayed in the document window.

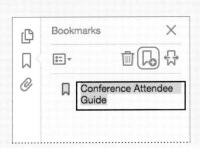

Moving bookmarks

After creating a bookmark, you can easily drag it to its proper place in the Bookmarks panel. You can move individual bookmarks or groups of bookmarks up and down in the Bookmarks panel, and you can nest bookmarks.

Some of the bookmarks are out of order in the current document. You'll rearrange them now.

1   In the Bookmarks panel, drag the icon for the Welcome bookmark directly below the icon for the Table of contents bookmark.

2   Drag the other bookmarks so that they appear in the same order as the entries in the table of contents.

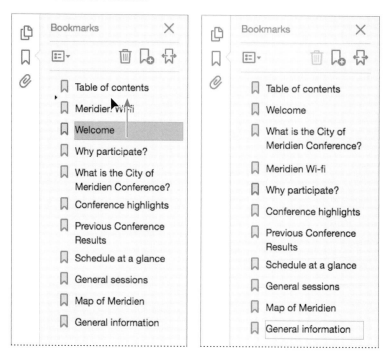

3   Close the Bookmarks panel, and then choose File > Save to save your work.

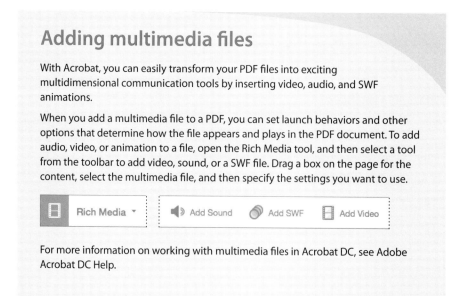

Adding multimedia files

With Acrobat, you can easily transform your PDF files into exciting multidimensional communication tools by inserting video, audio, and SWF animations.

When you add a multimedia file to a PDF, you can set launch behaviors and other options that determine how the file appears and plays in the PDF document. To add audio, video, or animation to a file, open the Rich Media tool, and then select a tool from the toolbar to add video, sound, or a SWF file. Drag a box on the page for the content, select the multimedia file, and then specify the settings you want to use.

For more information on working with multimedia files in Acrobat DC, see Adobe Acrobat DC Help.

Setting document properties and metadata

You're nearly done with this conference guide. To finish it off, you'll set the initial view, which determines what people see when they first open the file, and add metadata to the document.

1 Choose File > Properties.

2 In the Document Properties dialog box, click the Initial View tab.

3 From the Navigation Tab menu, choose Bookmarks Panel And Page.

When the viewer opens the file, both the page and the bookmarks will be visible.

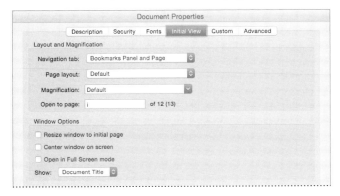

4 In the Window Options area, choose Document Title from the Show menu.

With this option selected, the document title, rather than the filename, will appear in the document's title bar.

5 Select the Description tab.

The document's author has already entered some metadata for the file, including some keywords. Metadata is information about the document itself, and you can use it to search for documents. You'll add some more keywords.

6 In the Keywords field, after the existing keywords, type **; map; vendors**. Keywords must be separated by commas or semicolons.

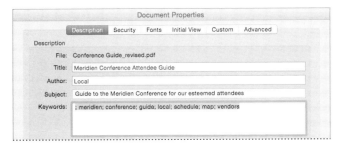

7 Click OK to accept changes in the Document Properties dialog box.

8 Choose File > Save to save your work, and then close all open files and quit Acrobat.

Setting up presentations

Generally, when you make a presentation to a group of people, you want the document to take over the entire screen, hiding distractions such as the menu bar, toolbars, and other window controls.

You can set up any PDF file to display in Full Screen mode in the Initial View tab of the Document Properties dialog box. In the Full Screen tab of the Preferences dialog box, you can set a variety of transition effects to play as you move between pages. You can even set the speed at which pages advance. You can also convert presentations that you've prepared in other programs, such as PowerPoint, to Adobe PDF, preserving many of the authoring program's special effects. For more information, see Adobe Acrobat DC Help.

Review questions

1 How can you change the order of pages in a PDF document?

2 How do you insert an entire PDF file into another PDF file?

3 How can you correct a link's destination?

4 What is a bookmark?

Review answers

1 You can change the page order by dragging the page thumbnails corresponding to the pages you want to move to their new locations in the Page Thumbnails panel.

2 To insert all the pages from a PDF file before or after any page in another PDF file, select the Organize Pages tool, choose Insert > From File, and then select the file you want to insert. Specify where in the document the pages should be inserted.

3 To correct a link's destination, select the Edit PDF tool, and then choose Link > Add Or Edit. Next, double-click the incorrect link. Then click the Actions tab in the Link Properties dialog box, click Edit, and type the correct page number in the Page box in the Go To A Page In This Document dialog box. Click OK.

4 A bookmark is simply a link represented by text in the Bookmarks panel.

5 EDITING CONTENT IN PDF FILES

Lesson overview

In this lesson, you'll do the following:

- Edit text in a PDF document.

- Add text to a PDF file.

- Add and replace images in a PDF file.

- Edit images in a PDF document.

- Copy text and images from a PDF document.

- Export PDF content to a Word, Excel, or PowerPoint document.

- Learn about redacting content.

 This lesson will take approximately an hour to complete. Copy the Lesson05 folder onto your hard drive if you haven't already done so.

globalcorp

Facilities Services Management Training

Linda White
WW Facilities Manager

With Acrobat DC, you can edit text and other PDF content smoothly and easily. You can also repurpose text, data, and images by copying or exporting content to another application.

Editing text

▶ **Tip:** As you can see, it's easy to make changes to a PDF document. If you want to ensure that your PDF file remains as you intended, apply security settings. For more on security, see Lesson 8, "Adding Signatures and Security."

In Acrobat DC, you can easily make simple and not-so-simple edits to text in PDF documents, as long as security settings permit it. Whether you're correcting typos, adding punctuation, or restructuring entire paragraphs, Acrobat reflows the text appropriately. You can even use the find-and-replace feature to correct or update multiple instances of a word or phrase in the PDF file. In addition to changes to content, you can edit text attributes such as spacing, point size, and color. If you attempt to change text in a font that is not available on your system, Acrobat prompts you to select a substitute font, and then remembers the substitution later.

Editing a single text block

You'll start by deleting unnecessary text in a document, and then you'll edit a paragraph to make it parallel with other bullet points.

1   Start Acrobat, and choose File > Open. Navigate to the Lesson05 folder, and double-click the Globalcorp_facilities.pdf file.

The Globalcorp_facilities.pdf file is an 18-page document that describes the responsibilities of a department at a fictitious company.

2   Go to page 3 in the document.

The document includes several sections, each with a headline such as "Office Services." Only page 3 includes a subhead ("Things to consider"). You'll delete the text so that it's consistent with the other section pages.

3   Click Edit PDF in the Tools pane.

By default, when you open the Edit PDF tool, Edit is selected in the Edit PDF toolbar, so bounding boxes appear around text blocks and images that are editable.

4   Click the "Things to consider" bounding box to select it, and then press the Delete key to remove it.

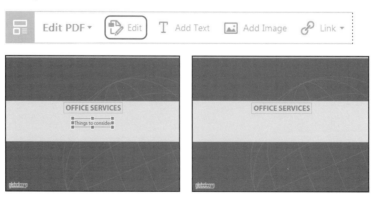

5 Go to page 11, which includes bullet points about furniture.

You'll change the second bullet point to start with a verb, making it parallel with all the other bullet points in the document.

6 Select "Purchases of new furniture need prior approval by."

7 Type **Obtain approval from**.

8 Click an insertion point after "Corporate," and type **before purchasing furniture.**

 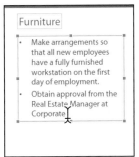 

Note: If you're unable to select text in a PDF file, the text may be part of an image. You can convert image text to text that can be selected by using the Recognize Text panel. For more information about text recognition, see Lesson 2, "Creating Adobe PDF files."

As you delete, replace, or add text, Acrobat reflows the paragraph.

9 Choose File > Save As, and save the file as **Globalcorp_facilities_edited.pdf** in the Lesson05 folder.

Replacing multiple occurrences of text

Acrobat DC includes a find-and-replace feature that is similar to one you might have used in a word processing or page layout application. You'll use it to replace the word "interface" with the word "communicate" throughout the document.

1 Choose Edit > Find.

2 In the Find panel, type **Interface** in the Find box, and then click Replace With to expand the panel.

3 Type **Communicate** in the Replace With box.

4 Click Next in the Find panel. Acrobat highlights the next occurrence of the word "interface," on page 10.

Tip: The Find feature is not case-sensitive.

5   Click Replace in the Find panel to replace the word.

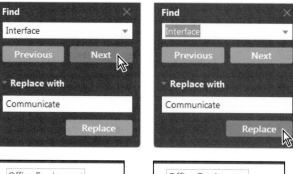

6   Click Next to locate the next occurrence, which is on the same page.

7   Click Replace, and then click Next again. Acrobat reports that it has found
all the instances of the word. Click OK to close the dialog box.

8   Close the Find panel.

Changing text properties

You can change the font, size, type style, alignment, and other attributes of text
without leaving Acrobat.

1   Go to page 2, and select the word "Agenda."

2   In the Format area of the right-hand pane, click the color swatch, select a new color,
and then close the Colors panel. We used magenta.

3 With the word "Agenda" still selected, click the Bold icon in the Format area.

4 Save your changes so far.

Adding text

You can also add entirely new blocks of text, including new bullet points. You'll add a bullet point to page 11.

1 Go to page 11.

2 Click an insertion point after the period in the second bullet item, and press Enter or Return.

Acrobat creates a new bullet and insertion point indented to match the previous bulleted items.

3 Type **Evaluate ergonomic needs and identify solutions.**

The formatting of the new bullet item matches the previous items.

▶ **Tip:** With the bounding box selected, you can resize items or move them anywhere on the page.

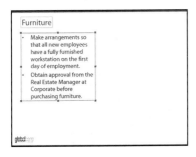
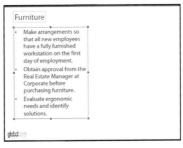

4 Go to page 18.

You'll add text to this page.

5 Select the bounding box that contains the words "Thank you!," and drag it closer to the top of the blue horizontal stripe.

6 Click Add Text in the Edit PDF toolbar.

7 Click a text insertion point directly below the "T" in "Thank you," and type **We look forward to working with you!**

The text appears with the formatting options that are currently selected in the right-hand pane. It matches the existing text on the page.

8 Select the text you just typed, and reduce the font size to 22. If necessary, move the text box to reposition it.

9 Save your work so far.

Redacting text
(Acrobat Pro only)

When courts make documents public or companies are required to produce documents that contain potentially confidential or privileged information, such information is often redacted, or hidden. In Acrobat Pro, you can use the Redact tool to automatically search for and permanently remove any privileged information.

You can search for specific terms, such as names, telephone numbers, or account numbers; you can also search for common patterns. You can redact information using the simple equivalent of a black marker, or add overlay text that identifies the privilege asserted, applicable statutory or code citation, or other basis for the redaction.

For information about using the Redact tool, see Adobe Acrobat Pro DC Help.

Working with images in a PDF file

In Acrobat DC, you can make simple changes to the position or size of an image in a PDF file, add images, or replace images. To make more substantial edits to an image, you can open it in an image-editing application such as Adobe Photoshop, and save it so that Acrobat updates the image in the PDF file.

Replacing images

It's easy to replace an image in a PDF file in Acrobat DC. You'll replace the image on page 4.

1   Go to page 4 in the Globalcorp_facilities_edited.pdf file.

2   Select Edit in the Edit PDF toolbar, if it's not already selected.

Note: Replacement images may not be the same size as the original image. You may want to adjust the dimensions or aspect ratio of an image before using it in your PDF document.

3   Right-click (Windows) or Control-click (Mac OS) the image of the cubicle, and choose Replace Image. Alternatively, you can select the image, and then click the Replace Image icon in the Format area of the right-hand pane.

4   In the Open dialog box, navigate to the Lesson05 folder, select the New_Reception.jpg file, and click Open.

Acrobat replaces the original image with the one you selected.

Adding images

You can also add images to a PDF file. You'll add one to the page that describes mail services.

1   Go to page 5.

2   Select Add Image in the Edit PDF toolbar.

3   In the Open dialog box, navigate to the Lesson05 folder, select the Boxes.jpg file, and click Open.

A thumbnail of the image is attached to the cursor.

4 Click on the right side of the page to place the image. Its upper left corner is aligned with the cursor's position at the time you clicked. You can drag the image to a different position.

Editing an image in Acrobat

Acrobat is not an image-editing application, but you can make some simple changes to your images without leaving Acrobat. You can rotate, flip, or crop an image in a PDF file.

1 On page 5, select the image of people with boxes.

2 Click the Crop icon (⛏.) in the Format area of the right-hand pane. The image handles change to look like old-fashioned photo corners.

3 Drag the lower right corner up to crop out much of the extra floor and the people to the right of the railing.

4 Drag the lower left corner up to the right, cropping out the people on the far left. The image should clearly focus on the three people in the center now. You can adjust the crop at the top of the image if you want to, or reposition it on either side.

5 Click the Crop icon again to deselect it. If you want to, you can drag the image to reposition it on the page and drag a corner handle to resize it so that it is more aesthetically pleasing.

6 Save the PDF file.

Editing an image in another application

If you want to lighten or darken an image, change its resolution, apply filters, or otherwise make substantive edits to it, you can edit it in an image-editing application. In this exercise, you'll make changes to the background image.

1 Select Edit in the Edit PDF toolbar if it's not already selected.

2 Still on page 5, select the background image for the entire page.

3 Choose an application from the Edit Using menu in the Format area of the right-hand pane.

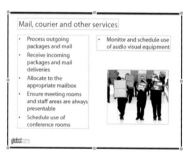 

Acrobat lists image-editing applications, such as Adobe Photoshop or Microsoft Paint, that are installed on your system. How extensively you can edit the image depends on the application you open it with.

4   Make changes to the image. For example, you can draw a red box or something equally obvious. Or, you can make a change that fits within the context of the document. Then save or close the image, depending on the application.

5   Return to Acrobat.

The changes you made appear on the page and will be saved with the PDF file. However, the original image (Boxes.jpg) is unchanged.

6   Close the Edit PDF tool and return to Document mode.

Copying text and images from a PDF file

Even if you no longer have access to the source file for a PDF document, you can reuse the text and images in other applications. For example, you might want to add some of the text or images to a web page. You can copy the text out of the PDF file in rich text format (RTF) or as accessible text so you can import it into a different authoring application for reuse. You can save images from the file in JPEG, TIF, or PNG format.

▶ **Tip:** You can change the security settings to prevent people from copying text or images from your PDF file. See Lesson 8, "Adding Signatures and Security."

If you want to reuse only small amounts of text or one or two images, copy them to the clipboard or to an image format file using the Selection tool. (If the Copy, Cut, and Paste commands are unavailable, the creator of the PDF may have set restrictions on editing the content of the document.)

You'll copy the text from a page in the facilities document for reuse.

1   Go to page 17.

2   Move the pointer over the text on the page. Notice that the pointer changes to an I-beam when it is in text-selection mode.

3   Drag the Selection tool across all the text on the page.

4   Right-click or Control-click the text, and choose Copy With Formatting, which preserves the layout.

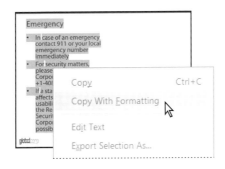

Note: Make sure you closed the Edit PDF tool. If you select text with the Edit option selected, you'll see different options in the context menu.

5 Minimize the Acrobat window, open a new or existing document in an authoring application such as a text editor or Microsoft Word, and then choose Edit > Paste.

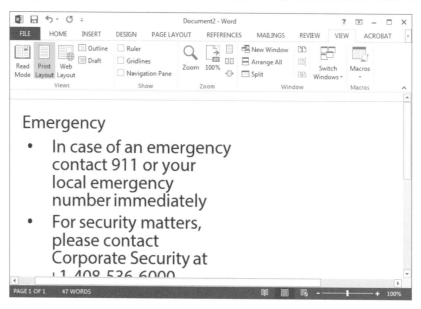

▶ **Tip:** You can also copy text and images from all or part of a page using the Snapshot feature. Choose Edit > Take A Snapshot, select the area you want to copy, click OK to close the message box, and then paste the image into another application. The resulting image is in bitmap format; any text it copies is not editable.

Your text is copied into the document in your authoring application, with most of the formatting from the PDF file. In most cases, you'll need to edit and format the text a little bit. If a font copied from a PDF document is not available on the system displaying the copied text, Acrobat substitutes the font.

You can save individual images for use in another application.

6 Go to page 4 in the document, and select the image.

7 Right-click (Windows) or Control-click (Mac OS) the image, and choose Save Image As.

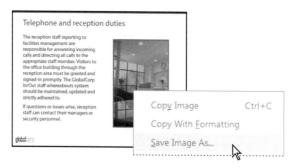

8 In the Save Image As dialog box, name the image **Reception Copy**, and choose JPEG from the Save As Type (Windows) or Format (Mac OS) menu. Save the file in the Lesson05 folder.

9   Close any open documents in other applications, but leave the Globalcorp_
    facilities_edited.pdf file open in Acrobat.

You've copied text from a PDF document, and you've saved an image for reuse.
You can also select both images and text, copy them, and paste them into another
application.

Exporting PDF content to a PowerPoint presentation

In Acrobat DC, you can export a PDF file as a Microsoft PowerPoint presentation.
Each page of the PDF document becomes a fully editable slide in PowerPoint,
retaining formatting and layout as much as possible.

You'll export the facilities document to a PowerPoint presentation.

1   With the Globalcorp_facilities_edited.pdf file open, click Export PDF in the Tools
    pane, and then select Microsoft PowerPoint for the format.

2   Click Export.

Note: You can specify whether to include comments and whether to run OCR to recognize text when you save as a PowerPoint presentation. To change the settings, choose Edit > Preferences (Windows) or Acrobat > Preferences (Mac OS), select Convert From PDF from the list on the left, select PowerPoint Presentation from the Converting From PDF list, and then click Edit Settings.

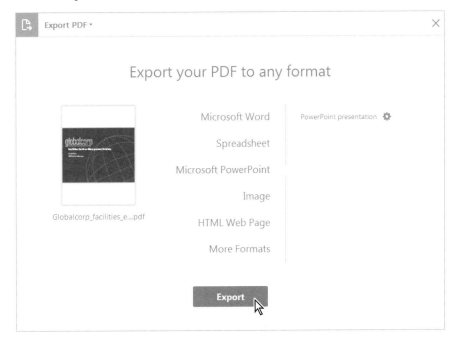

Export PDF ▾

Export your PDF to any format

Microsoft Word

Spreadsheet

Microsoft PowerPoint

Image

HTML Web Page

More Formats

PowerPoint presentation ⚙

Globalcorp_facilities_e....pdf

Export

▶ Tip: If you have a Document Cloud subscription, you can export PDF files to Word, PowerPoint, or Excel on a tablet or phone using the Acrobat DC mobile app. If you're using an iPad, you can also edit a PDF file. To learn more, see "Going mobile" on page 6.

3   In the Export dialog box, select the Lesson05 folder, and then click Save.

4   Preview the presentation in PowerPoint, if it's installed. If you do not have PowerPoint installed, you may be able to preview the presentation using the Preview application in Mac OS.

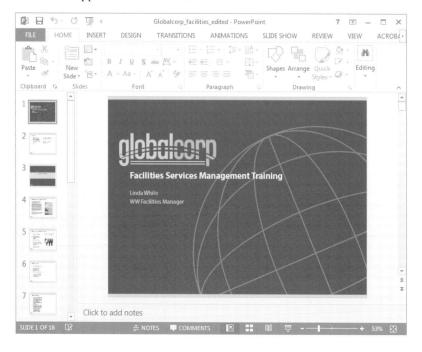

Some text and images may have shifted. When you export a PDF file to a PowerPoint presentation, evaluate each slide carefully, and make any necessary adjustments in PowerPoint.

5   Close the Globalcorp_facilities_edited.pdf file, and PowerPoint or any other applications that are open. Leave Acrobat open.

Saving PDF files as Word documents

You can save PDF files as Word documents (either .docx or .doc files), no matter what application the document originated in. You'll save a statement of work for a fictitious company as a Word document.

1   In Acrobat, choose File > Open. Navigate to the Lesson05 folder, and select the Statement_of_Work.pdf file. Click Open.

2   Choose File > Export To > Microsoft Word > Word Document. (If you're using Word 2003 or earlier, choose Word 97-2003 Document, which saves a .doc file.)

3   In the Save As dialog box, click Settings.

4   In the Save As DOC Settings or Save As DOCX Settings dialog box, select Retain Page Layout. Make sure the other options are all selected. Then click OK.

5   Click Save to save the file.

▶ **Tip:** You can save PDF files as PowerPoint presentations, Word documents, or Excel spreadsheets by choosing an option in the Export PDF tool, choosing File > Export To > [format], or choosing an option from the Save As Type or Format menu in the Save As PDF dialog box.

Acrobat displays the status of the conversion process as it works. When you save complex PDF documents, the conversion to Word may take longer. If View Result was selected in the Save As PDF dialog box, the document automatically opens in Word or a similar application.

6   Open the Statement_of_Work.doc or Statement_of_Work.docx file in Word, if it's not already open. You may also be able to open the document in Preview or Pages in Mac OS, or in another application that can open .doc or .docx files.

7 Scroll through the document to confirm that the text and images have been saved appropriately.

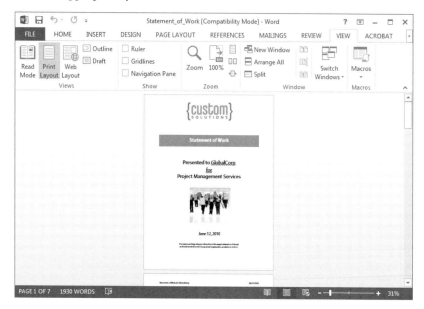

In most cases, Acrobat saves PDF files as Word documents with impressive integrity. However, depending on the way the document was created, you may need to adjust spacing or make minor corrections. Always carefully review a document in Word after you've saved it from Acrobat.

8 Close the PDF file in Acrobat, and then quit Word or any other applications.

Extracting PDF tables as Excel spreadsheets

You can export an entire PDF file or selected tables as Excel worksheets. You'll export a list of restaurants from a PDF document to a new Excel file.

1   In Acrobat, choose File > Open. Navigate to the Lesson05 folder, and select Venues.pdf. Click Open.

The PDF document includes a table of restaurants in the fictitious city of Meridien. You'll export that table to an Excel file.

2   Drag from the upper left corner of the table to the lower right corner, so that the entire table is selected.

3   Right-click or Control-click the selected table, and choose Export Selection As.

 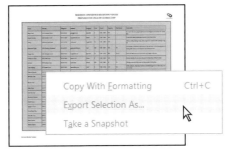

4   In the Export Selection As dialog box, choose Excel Workbook from the Save As Type or Format menu. Name the file **Venues.xlsx**. Then click Save.

Acrobat reports its progress. If View Result was selected in the Export Selection As dialog box, your new spreadsheet opens in Excel or another application automatically.

5   Open the Venues.xlsx file if it isn't already open. You may also be able to open the file in Preview in Mac OS or in other applications that can open Excel documents.

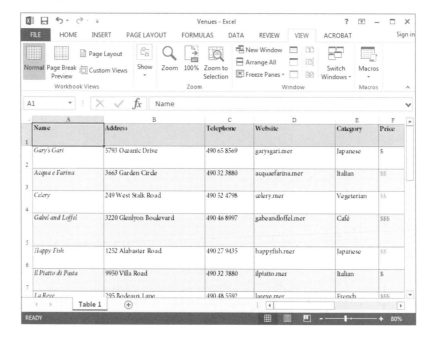

Acrobat appropriately converted the fields in the table.

6   Close any open documents, Acrobat, and other applications.

Review questions

1 How do you edit text in a PDF file?

2 How can you prevent others from editing or reusing content in a PDF file?

3 What kinds of edits can you make to an image in Acrobat?

4 How can you export a PDF file to Microsoft Word, Microsoft Excel, or Microsoft PowerPoint format?

5 How do you copy text from a PDF file?

Review answers

1 To edit text in a PDF file, select Edit PDF in the Tools pane, make sure Edit is selected in the Edit PDF toolbar, and then make your edits. Acrobat reflows the text as you change it.

2 To prevent others from editing or reusing the content of your PDF file, apply security to the document.

3 You can rotate, flip, crop, resize, or replace an image in Acrobat.

4 To export a PDF file to Word, Excel, or PowerPoint format, do one of the following:

- Choose an option from the Export PDF tool.

- Choose File > Export To > [format].

- Choose an option from the Save As Type or Format menu in the Save As PDF dialog box.

5 If you're copying a couple of words or sentences, right-click or Control-click the selected text, and choose Copy With Formatting to retain the formatting when you paste the text.

6 USING ACROBAT WITH MICROSOFT OFFICE FILES (WINDOWS)

Lesson overview

In this lesson, you'll do the following:

- Convert a Microsoft Word file to Adobe PDF.

- Convert Word headings and styles to PDF bookmarks.

- Convert Word comments to PDF notes.

- Change the Adobe PDF conversion settings.

- Convert a Microsoft Excel file to Adobe PDF.

- Use the spreadsheet split view.

- Convert a Microsoft PowerPoint presentation to Adobe PDF.

 This lesson will take approximately 45 minutes to complete. Copy the Lesson06 folder onto your hard drive if you haven't already done so.

Statement of Work
for
Local

Meridien Conference
Promotion Program

Presented by

GlobalCorp
April 22, 2015

Using Acrobat PDFMaker, you can easily convert
Microsoft Office documents to PDF. PDFMaker settings let you convert Word headings to bookmarks,
include comments, and start email-based reviews.

Getting started

▶ **Tip:** To create PDF files from Office documents in Mac OS, see Lesson 2, "Creating Adobe PDF Files."

This lesson is designed for Windows users who have Microsoft Office 2007 or later applications such as Microsoft Word, Microsoft PowerPoint, and Microsoft Excel installed on their computers. You need to have one or more of these applications installed on your system to complete the exercises. If you do not use these Microsoft Office applications, skip this lesson. Visit the Adobe website (www.adobe.com) to see which versions of Microsoft Office are supported.

This lesson assumes you are using Microsoft Office 2013, but the steps are similar in earlier versions.

About Acrobat PDFMaker

Acrobat PDFMaker makes it easy to convert Microsoft Office documents to PDF. When you install Acrobat in Windows, it automatically installs PDFMaker for supported Microsoft Office applications (Microsoft Office 2007, 2010, and 2013) it finds on the system. PDFMaker options are available on the Acrobat ribbon. You can control the settings used in the PDF conversion, automatically email the PDF file, and set up an email review process without ever leaving the Microsoft application. PDFMaker can also attach your Office source file to the PDF file.

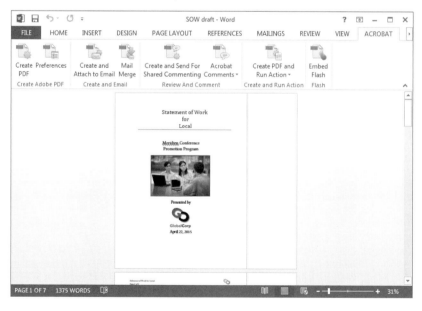

PDF files are often substantially smaller than their source files. You can also create PDF/A-compliant files from Office files.

If you don't see the Acrobat ribbon, choose File > Options, select Add-Ins in the Options dialog box, and select Acrobat PDFMaker Office COM Addin. Then close and restart your Microsoft application.

Acrobat installs essentially the same buttons and commands in Word, PowerPoint, and Excel. There are, however, some application-specific differences.

Converting Microsoft Word files to Adobe PDF

Word is a popular authoring program that makes it easy to create a variety of types of documents. Word documents often include text styles and hyperlinks, and they may contain comments added during a review process. When you create an Adobe PDF document from your Word document, you can convert text using specific Word styles, such as headings, to Acrobat bookmarks, and you can convert comments to Acrobat notes. Hyperlinks in a Word document are preserved when it is converted to PDF. Your Adobe PDF file will look just like your Word file and retain the same functionality, but it will be equally accessible to readers on all platforms, regardless of whether they have the Word application. PDF files created from Word files can also be tagged, making the content easy to repurpose, and improving accessibility.

▶ **Tip:** If you have a Document Cloud subscription, you can convert Microsoft Office files to PDF on a tablet or phone using the Acrobat DC mobile app. To learn more, see "Going mobile" on page 6.

Converting Word headings and styles to PDF bookmarks

If your Word document contains headings and styles that you want to convert to linked bookmarks in Adobe PDF, you must identify these headings and styles in the Acrobat PDFMaker dialog box. (Word Heading 1 through Heading 9 styles are converted automatically.) You'll convert a statement of work document that was formatted using custom styles. You'll need to make sure that the styles used are converted to linked bookmarks when you create the Adobe PDF file.

1 Start Microsoft Word.

2 In Word, choose File > Open. Navigate to the Lesson06 folder, select the SOW draft.doc file, and click Open. Choose File > Save As, rename the file **SOW draft_final.doc**, and save it in the Lesson06 folder.

First, you'll change the PDF settings to create bookmarks based on the styles used in the document.

3 Click Acrobat to open the Acrobat ribbon, and then click Preferences.

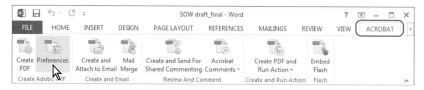

The Acrobat PDFMaker dialog box contains the settings that control the PDF conversion. There are different tabs available, depending on the application. In Word, the dialog box includes a Word tab and a Bookmarks tab.

4 Click the Bookmarks tab to select which styles are used to create bookmarks.

5 Scroll down the list, and select the Bookmark option for each of the following styles: Second Level, Third Level, Title, and Top Level. These are the styles you want to use to create bookmarks.

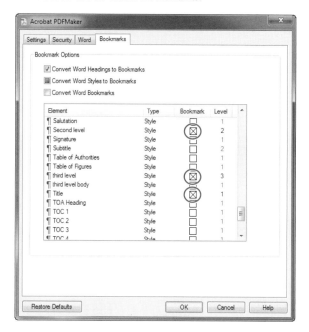

Notice that the level for Title and Top Level is automatically set to 1, Second Level is set to 2, and Third Level is set to 3. These are the hierarchical levels of PDF bookmarks. To change the level setting for a style, click its level number, and then choose a new level from the pop-up menu.

Any settings that you make in the Bookmarks tab apply only to the conversion of Word documents.

Converting Word comments to PDF notes

You needn't lose any comments that have been added to your Word document when you convert the document to Adobe PDF: You can convert them to PDF notes. There are two comments in this document that need to remain available in the PDF.

1   Click the Word tab in the Acrobat PDFMaker dialog box, and select Convert Displayed Comments To Notes In Adobe PDF.

The Comments area displays information about the comments that will be included. Make sure that the box in the Include column is selected.

2   To change the color of the note in the Adobe PDF document, click repeatedly on the icon in the Color column to cycle through the available color choices. We chose blue.

3   To have the note automatically open in the PDF document, select the Notes Open option. You can always close the note in the PDF document later if you wish.

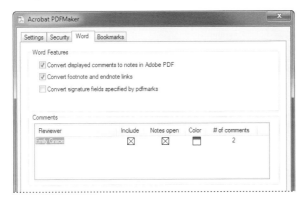

Any settings that you make in the Word tab apply only to the conversion of Word documents.

Specifying the conversion settings

In every Office application, PDFMaker includes the Settings tab, which is where you can select the conversion settings that determine how the PDF file is created. For most purposes, the predefined settings files (or presets) work well. However, if you need to customize the conversion settings, click Advanced Settings, and then make the changes appropriate for your file.

You'll convert this document using the Standard settings file.

1   Click the Settings tab.

2   From the Conversion Settings menu, choose Standard.

3 Verify that View Adobe PDF Result is selected. When this option is selected, Acrobat automatically displays the Adobe PDF file you create as soon as the conversion is complete.

4 Make sure that Create Bookmarks is selected.

5 Make sure that Enable Accessibility And Reflow With Tagged Adobe PDF is selected. Tagging PDF files makes them more accessible.

For more information on making your PDF files accessible, see Lesson 3, "Reading and Working with PDF Files."

● **Note:** Acrobat PDFMaker will use these conversion settings for converting Word documents until you change them.

6 Select Attach Source File to attach the Word document to the PDF file. This option can be useful if you want the viewer to have access to the original for editing purposes.

7 Click OK to apply your settings.

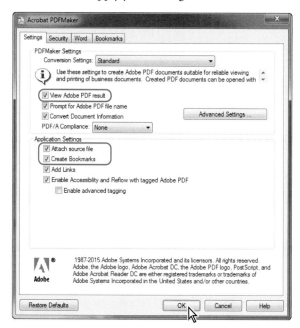

8 Choose File > Save to save your work so far.

Converting your Word file

Now that you've defined the settings to be used for the conversion, you're ready to convert your Word file to Adobe PDF.

1 Click the Create PDF button on the Acrobat ribbon.

2 In the Save Adobe PDF As dialog box, name the file **SOW draft.pdf**, and save it in the Lesson06 folder.

PDFMaker converts the Word document to Adobe PDF. The status of the conversion is shown in the Acrobat PDFMaker message box.

Because you selected View Adobe PDF Result, Acrobat automatically displays your converted file. Notice that the Word comment has been converted to an open Adobe PDF note.

3 Scroll if necessary to see the first note. After you have read the sticky note, click the close button on the sticky note.

▶ **Tip:** In Acrobat DC, you can edit headers and footers in PDF files created from Office 2007 and later files.

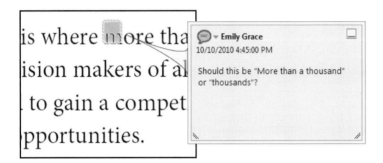

4 Click the Bookmarks button (🔖) in the navigation pane, and view the bookmarks that were created automatically.

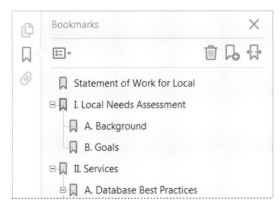

In Acrobat DC, when you select a bookmark in the navigation pane, the link takes you directly to the heading, not the top of the page that contains the heading.

5 Click the Attachments button (✐) in the navigation pane to verify that your original Word file is attached.

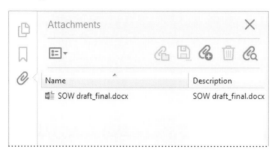

▶ **Tip:** If you simply want to convert your Microsoft Office file to Adobe PDF using the current PDFMaker conversion settings, drag the Office file onto the Acrobat DC icon on your desktop or into an empty document pane in the Acrobat work area.

6 When you have finished reviewing the file, close it.

7 Choose File > Exit to quit Acrobat.

8 Quit Microsoft Word.

Creating Adobe PDF files from Word mail-merge templates

Word mail-merges generate documents such as form letters, which are personalized with the names and addresses of the individuals to whom they will be sent. With Acrobat PDFMaker, you can use a Word mail-merge template and its corresponding data file to output mail-merges directly to PDF. You can even set up PDFMaker to attach those PDF files to email messages that are generated during the PDF-creation process. Click the Mail Merge button in the Acrobat ribbon to start the process. For more information, see Adobe Acrobat DC Help.

Converting Excel documents

When you convert Excel documents to PDF, you can easily select and order the worksheets you want to include, retain all links, and create bookmarks. You'll create an Adobe PDF file from an Excel document after customizing the conversion settings.

Converting the entire workbook

You can choose to convert an entire workbook, a selection, or selected sheets to PDF. In this exercise, you'll convert an entire workbook.

1 Start Microsoft Excel.

2 Depending on your version, click Open Other Workbooks, or choose File > Open. Then, navigate to the Lesson06 folder, select the Financials.xls file, and click Open. Then choose File > Save As, rename the file **Financials_final.xls**, and save it in the Lesson06 folder.

This Excel file includes two worksheets. The first lists construction costs, and the second shows operating costs. You'll need to convert both of these sheets to include them in the PDF. You'll start by changing the PDF conversion settings.

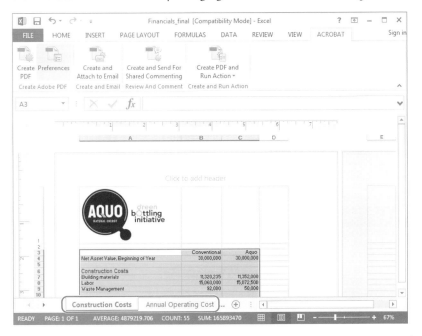

3 Click Preferences in the Acrobat ribbon.

4 In the Settings tab of the Acrobat PDFMaker dialog box, choose Smallest File Size from the Conversion Settings menu, because you're going to be emailing the PDF file.

5 Select the Fit Worksheet To A Single Page option.

6 Make sure that the Enable Accessibility And Reflow With Tagged Adobe PDF option is selected. When you create tagged PDF, you can more easily copy tabular data from PDF files back into spreadsheet applications. Creating tagged PDF also makes your files more accessible.

7 Select the Prompt For Conversion Settings option to open a dialog box at the beginning of the file conversion process, which will allow you to specify which sheets to include and in what order.

PDFMaker will use these conversion settings when converting Excel documents to PDF until you change the settings.

8 Click OK to apply your settings.

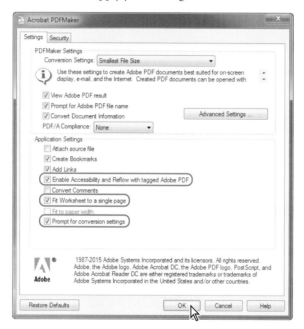

In Acrobat, you can convert an oversized worksheet to a PDF that is one sheet wide and several sheets long. In the Settings tab of the Acrobat PDFMaker dialog box, the Fit Worksheet To A Single Page option adjusts the size of each worksheet so that all the entries on that worksheet appear on the same page of the PDF. The Fit To Paper Width option adjusts the width of each worksheet so that all the columns on that worksheet appear on one page in the PDF.

Creating the PDF file

You'll convert the Excel workbook to a PDF file. PDFMaker uses the settings you specified earlier.

1 Click the Create PDF button on the Acrobat ribbon.

2 In the Acrobat PDFMaker dialog box, select Entire Workbook.

This is the dialog box where you'd select specific material or worksheets, if you wanted to.

3 Click Convert To PDF.

4 In the Save Adobe PDF File As dialog box, click Save to save the file as **Financials_final.pdf** in the Lesson06 folder.

Acrobat opens the PDF document automatically if View Result was selected in the Save Adobe PDF File As dialog box.

5 Review the Financials_final.pdf file in Acrobat, and then close the PDF file and close Excel.

Using the spreadsheet split view

When you work with spreadsheets, it is often useful to be able to keep the column or row names in view while scrolling up and down columns or across rows. The Spreadsheet Split command in Acrobat lets you do this.

1 In Acrobat, choose File > Open. Navigate to the Lesson06 folder, and open the GE_Schedule.pdf file.

This schedule is difficult to read onscreen because the type size is small if you have the view set to Fit Page. You'll use the Spreadsheet Split command to look more closely at some of the data. First you'll change the view of the page.

2 Choose Window > Spreadsheet Split to divide the document pane into four quadrants.

You can drag the splitter bars up, down, left, or right to resize the panes.

In Spreadsheet Split view, changing the zoom level changes the magnification in all the quadrants. (In Split view, you can have a different zoom level in each of the two windows.)

3 Drag the vertical splitter bar so that the categories fill the left pane.

4 Drag the horizontal splitter bar so that it is directly below the column headings.

5 Use the vertical scroll bar to scroll down through the categories. Because the column headers remain visible, it is easy to evaluate the schedule for each task.

6 When you are finished exploring the Spreadsheet Split view, close the GE_Schedule.pdf file without saving your work.

Converting PowerPoint presentations

You can convert Microsoft PowerPoint presentations to PDF in the same way that you convert Microsoft Word documents. However, there are additional options available to help you preserve the look and feel of the presentation. You'll convert a simple presentation and preserve its slide transitions.

1 Start PowerPoint. Depending on the version of PowerPoint, click Open Other Presentations or choose File > Open. Then navigate to the Lesson06 folder, and select the Projector Setup.ppt file. Click Open.

A Push transition has been applied to the slides in this file.

2 Click Preferences in the Acrobat ribbon.

3 Select the Settings tab, and then select Convert Multimedia and Preserve Slide Transitions. Make sure View Adobe PDF Result is selected, too.

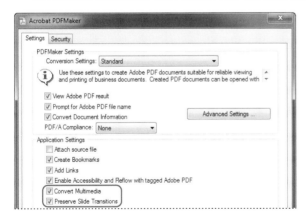

4 Click OK.

You can include speaker's notes and hidden slides, and specify other settings.

5 Click Create PDF in the Acrobat ribbon. Then click Save in the Save Adobe PDF dialog box. Acrobat opens the PDF file after conversion.

6 In Acrobat, choose View > Full Screen Mode. Then press the arrow keys to move through the presentation. The Push slide transitions remain in the PDF file. Press the Esc key to exit Full Screen Mode. Then, close the PDF file and PowerPoint.

Review questions

1 How can you be sure that Word styles and headings are converted to Acrobat bookmarks when you convert Word documents to Adobe PDF using PDFMaker?

2 How can you scroll through a spreadsheet in Acrobat without losing sight of the column headings?

3 Can you retain slide transitions when you save a PowerPoint presentation to PDF?

Review answers

1 If you want Word headings and styles to be converted to bookmarks in Acrobat, select them for conversion in the Acrobat PDFMaker dialog box. In Microsoft Word, click Preferences in the Acrobat ribbon (choose Adobe PDF > Change Conversion Settings in earlier versions of Word), and click the Bookmarks tab. Make sure that the required headings and styles are selected.

2 To see column headings while you review the content of a spreadsheet, choose Window > Spreadsheet Split, which divides the document pane into four quadrants. Move the divider bars where you want them, and then scroll through the rows.

3 Yes, you can retain slide transitions when you save a PowerPoint presentation to PDF. To do so, click Preferences in the Acrobat ribbon (or choose Adobe PDF > Change Conversion Settings in earlier versions of PowerPoint), and then make sure Preserve Slide Transitions is selected. PDFMaker uses those settings until you change them.

7 COMBINING FILES

Lesson overview

In this lesson, you'll do the following:

- Quickly and easily combine files of different types into one PDF document.

- Select individual pages to include in a combined PDF file.

- Customize a combined PDF file.

- Combine files into a PDF Portfolio (Acrobat Pro only).

 This lesson will take approximately 45 minutes to complete. Copy the Lesson07 folder onto your hard drive if you haven't already done so.

You can easily combine multiple files, including files of different file types, into a coherent PDF document. You can even select which pages to include from each document.

About combining files

In Acrobat DC, you can assemble multiple files into an integrated PDF document. You can combine files of different formats, created in different applications. As long as you have applications installed that support the native documents' formats, they'll automatically be converted to PDF. For example, you could assemble all the documents for a specific project, including text documents, email messages, spreadsheets, CAD drawings, and PowerPoint presentations. When you combine the files, you can select specific pages from each document and then rearrange them. Acrobat converts each to PDF and then assembles them into a single PDF file.

If you have Acrobat DC Pro, you can choose to combine files in a PDF Portfolio. Files in a PDF Portfolio do not need to be converted to PDF; they can remain in their original format but are assembled into a coherent document. For more information, see the sidebar "Creating a PDF Portfolio" at the end of this lesson.

Selecting files to combine

In this lesson, you'll create a combined PDF file that contains documents for the board meeting of a fictitious beverage company. You'll assemble several PDF files, a logo, a Microsoft Word document, a Microsoft PowerPoint presentation, and a Microsoft Excel spreadsheet. You can select which pages of each document to include in the combined PDF file.

NOTE: Acrobat requires the native application be installed in order to convert a document to PDF. If you do not have Word, Excel, or PowerPoint installed on your computer, you will not be able to include those files in your combined PDF. You can skip those files and complete the exercise without them.

Adding files

First, you'll select the files you want to include in the combined PDF file.

1 Start Acrobat.

2 Click Tools.

3 In the Tools Center, click the Combine Files tool. You may need to scroll down to see it.

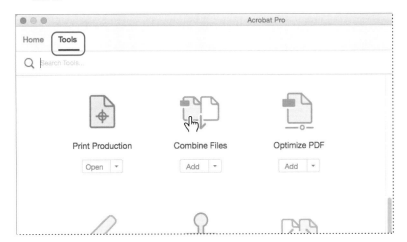

The Combine Files dialog box appears.

4 Click Add Files at the top of the dialog box, and then choose Add Files.

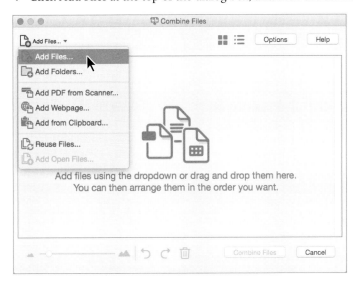

5 Navigate to the Lesson07 folder.

The folder contains a GIF file, an Excel spreadsheet, a PowerPoint presentation, a Word document, and several PDF files.

▶ Tip: Select the first file, and then Shift-click the last one to select all the files in the folder.

6   Select the following files, and click Open (Windows) or Add Files (Mac OS):

- Aquo_Bottle.pdf
- Aquo_Building.pdf
- Aquo_Costs.pdf
- Aquo_Fin_Ana.xls
- Aquo_Fin_Data.ppt
- Aquo_Mkt_Summ.doc
- Aquo_Overview.pdf
- Logo.gif

If you do not have the required software installed to convert a document, you won't be able to select it.

Browsing files

● Note: In Mac OS, the source applications (Microsoft Word, Excel, and PowerPoint) may open as you select the files. Acrobat uses the source applications to create the thumbnails it displays in the Combine Files dialog box.

Acrobat displays a thumbnail for each selected file in the Combine Files dialog box. You can use those thumbnails to preview a document, select specific pages to include, delete a file, or rearrange the pages in the final file.

1   Select the Aquo_Bottle.pdf thumbnail.

2   Move the cursor over the thumbnail. Acrobat displays the filename, size, modification date, and the number of pages it contains.

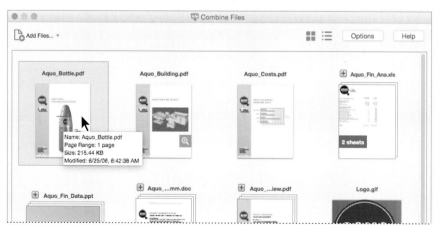

3 Click the magnifying glass on the thumbnail to zoom in to the full page.

4 Click anywhere in the dialog box to close the preview box.

5   Click the plus sign next to the Aquo_Overview.pdf filename to see each of the pages in the document.

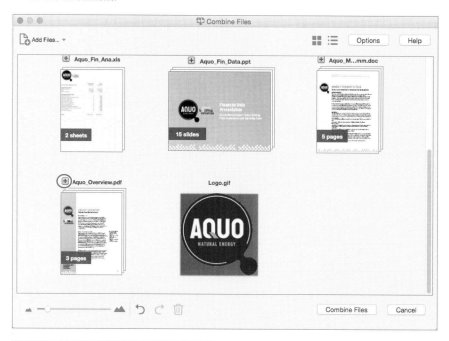

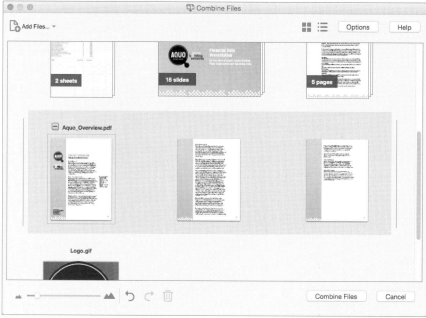

You can preview each page separately, rearrange them, or delete them from the combined PDF file.

6 Select the thumbnail of the third page in the Aquo_Overview.pdf file, and then click the Remove Selected Items button at the bottom of the dialog box.

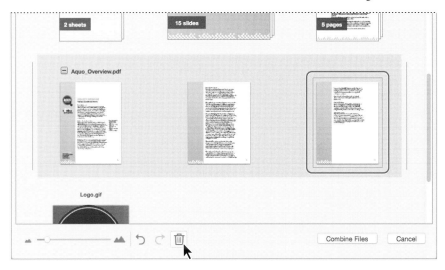

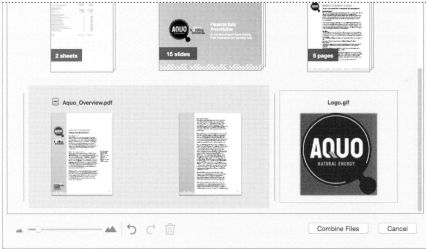

Only two pages remain in the document.

7 Click the minus sign next to the Aquo_Overview.pdf filename to collapse it back to a single thumbnail.

● Note: If you were not able to add the Aquo_Fin_Ana.xls file to the Combine Files dialog box, skip step 8.

8 Click the plus sign next to the Aquo_Fin_Ana.xls file to view the two worksheets it contains.

● **Note:** If you were not able to add the Aquo_Fin_Data.ppt file to the Combine Files dialog box, skip steps 9–11.

9 Click the plus sign next to the Aquo_Fin_Data.ppt file to expand its slides. If you can't see all the slides, move the slider at the bottom of the Combine Files window to reduce the size of the thumbnails.

10 Select the last six slides in the presentation, slides 10–15. (Hover over a thumbnail to see the slide number.)

11 Click the Remove Selected Items button at the bottom of the dialog box to omit the slides from the combined PDF file.

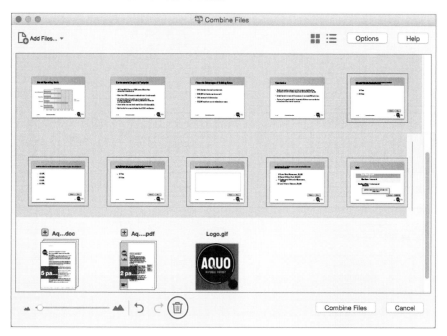

Arranging pages

You can organize the pages in the merged file before you actually create it. Just drag and drop thumbnails in the Combine Files dialog box to place them in the order you want them to appear.

1 Drag the Logo.gif file to the top of the dialog box, so that it's the first file, before Aquo_Bottle.pdf.

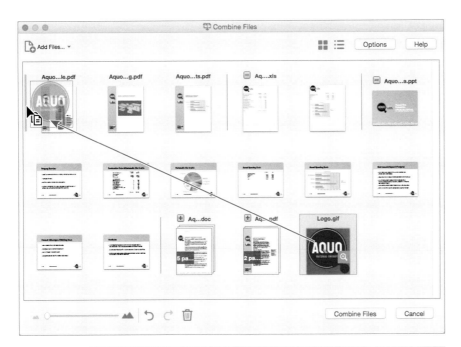

2   Drag the second slide in the Aquo_Fin_Data.ppt file so that it appears right after the Logo.gif file.

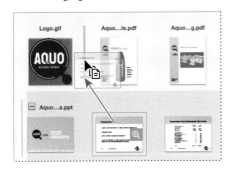 

Note: If you were unable to add the Aquo_Fin_Data.pptx file, skip step 2. Likewise, ignore any files in step 3 that don't appear in the Combine Files dialog box on your system.

You can arrange documents, or individual pages within those documents.

3 Collapse any expanded documents, and then arrange the remaining documents so that they appear in the following order:

- Logo.gif
- Slide 2 of Aquo_Fin_Data.ppt
- Aquo_Bottle.pdf
- Aquo_Overview.pdf
- Aquo_Building.pdf
- Aquo_Costs.pdf
- Aquo_Mkt_Summ.doc
- Aquo_Fin_Data.ppt
- Aquo_Fin_Ana.xls

4   Click the Switch To List button at the top of the dialog box to see the filenames and information instead of thumbnails.

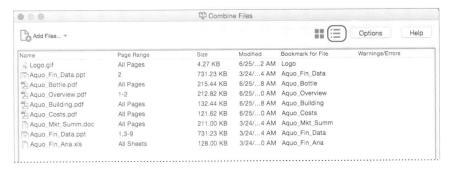

Merging the files

When you've selected the pages you want to include and arranged them in the appropriate order, you're ready to combine the files.

1   Click Options at the top of the Combine Files dialog box.

2   In the Options dialog box, make sure the Default File Size option and Single PDF are selected.

The Small File Size option uses compression and resolution settings that are appropriate for onscreen display. The Default File Size option creates PDF files for business printing and viewing onscreen. The Larger File Size option uses High Quality Print conversion settings.

The Single PDF option combines all the files into a single combined PDF document. The Portfolio option creates a PDF Portfolio.

3   Make sure Always Add Bookmarks To Adobe PDF Files is selected.

When this option is selected, Acrobat creates bookmarks for the file as it converts and combines the documents.

4   Click OK to close the Options dialog box.

5 Click Combine Files.

Acrobat reports its progress as it converts individual documents to PDF format and then combines the files. Some source applications may open and close during the conversion process. When Acrobat has finished merging the documents, it opens the resulting file, named Binder1.pdf.

6 Click the Bookmarks button in the navigation pane to view the bookmarks Acrobat created for the document.

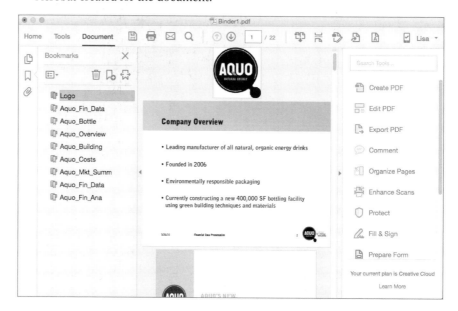

Because you moved a slide separately from the rest of the presentation, that document is included twice in the list of bookmarks. In Windows, Acrobat creates additional bookmarks for individual pages, nested under the bookmark for the document name. Depending on your goals for the document, you might want to edit the bookmarks.

7 Browse through the document. The pages are in the order you specified.

8 Choose File > Save As, and save the document as **Aquo presentation** in the Lesson07 folder.

9 Close the Aquo presentation.pdf file.

Creating a PDF Portfolio (Acrobat Pro)

In Acrobat DC Pro, you can assemble files of different formats into a PDF Portfolio. You do not need to convert files into PDF to include them in a PDF Portfolio.

PDF Portfolios offer several advantages over files merged into an ordinary PDF file or native files stored separately:

- You can add and remove component documents easily.

- You can quickly preview component files without having to pause for Open or Save dialog boxes.

- You can edit individual files within the PDF Portfolio without affecting the other files. You can also edit non-PDF files in their native applications from within a PDF Portfolio; any changes you make are saved to the file within the PDF Portfolio.

- You can search the entire PDF Portfolio or individual component documents, including non-PDF component files.

- You can add non-PDF files to an existing PDF Portfolio without converting them to PDF.

To create a merged PDF Portfolio:

1 Choose File > Create > PDF Portfolio.

The Create PDF Portfolio dialog box is similar to the Combine Files dialog box.

2 Click Add Files at the top of the dialog box, and then choose Add Files.

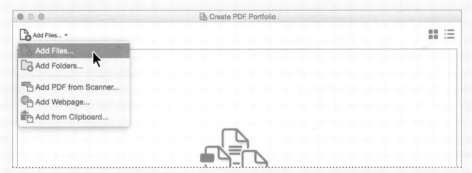

3 Select the files you want to include, and click Open (Windows) or Add Files (Mac OS).

4 Arrange the files or individual pages from them in the order you want them to appear in the PDF Portfolio. Delete any pages you don't want to include.

5 Click Create.

Acrobat opens the PDF Portfolio, named Portfolio.pdf. It lists the Portfolio components in the navigation pane on the left.

sidebar continues on next page

Creating a PDF Portfolio (Acrobat Pro) (continued)

To navigate the PDF Portfolio, click a component name on the left, use the Previous and Next buttons in the document taskbar, or press the Left and Right Arrow keys on your keyboard.

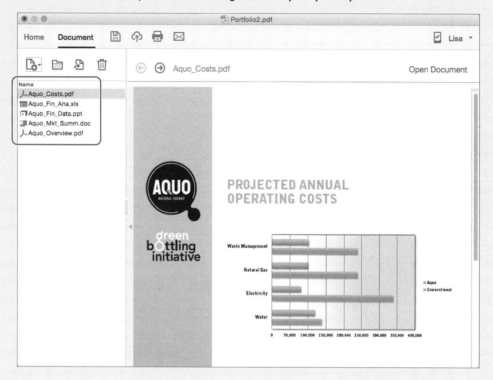

If the selected component is a non-PDF document, click Open Document in the upper right corner to open the document in its native application, such as Microsoft Word. If the selected document is a PDF file, clicking Open Document opens a separate copy of the PDF document.You can extract individual documents from a PDF Portfolio, whether they're PDF files or native documents. To extract a file, navigate to the document in the PDF Portfolio, and then choose File > Extract File From Portfolio. Name the file, choose a folder for it, and click Save.

6 Choose File > PDF Portfolio.

The Save As PDF dialog box opens.

7 Select a folder for the PDF Portfolio, and then name it, and click Save.

Review questions

1 Can you include documents in non-PDF formats in a combined PDF file?

2 How do you arrange pages in a combined PDF file?

3 Why would you want to preview or browse a file in the Combine Files dialog box?

4 Name one advantage of a PDF Portfolio.

Review answers

1 Yes, you can include documents in any format in a combined PDF file, as long as you have the application that created the document installed. Acrobat converts documents to PDF as it combines the files.

2 To arrange pages in a combined PDF file, drag their thumbnails in the Combine Files dialog box.

3 It's handy to be able to preview or browse files in the Combine Files dialog box so that you can determine whether you want to include each file or all the pages of a file, and in which order.

4 PDF Portfolios provide several advantages:

    • You can add and remove component documents easily, including non-PDF files.

    • You can preview component files quickly.

    • You can edit individual files within the PDF Portfolio independently.

    • PDF Portfolios contain all their components, so you can share them easily.

    • You can search the entire PDF Portfolio, including non-PDF component files.

8 ADDING SIGNATURES AND SECURITY

Lesson overview

In this lesson, you'll do the following:

- Use Acrobat Reader in Protected Mode (Windows only).

- Apply password protection to a file to restrict who can open it.

- Apply a password to prevent others from printing or changing a PDF file.

- Use Document Cloud eSign Services to send documents for digital signatures.

- Create a digital ID that includes an image.

- Sign documents using a digital ID.

- Certify a document.

 This lesson will take approximately 45 minutes to complete. Copy the Lesson08 folder onto your hard drive if you haven't already done so.

{custom}
SOLUTIONS

Statement of Work

Presented to GlobalCorp
for
Project Management Services

June 12, 2015

The names and logo designs referred to in this sample artwork are fictional
and not intended to refer to any actual organization, products or services.

You can keep your PDF documents secure through
password protection, certification, and digital
signatures.

Getting started

Acrobat DC provides several tools to help you secure your PDF documents. You can use passwords to prevent unauthorized users from opening, printing, or editing PDF files. You can use a certificate to encrypt PDF documents so that only an approved list of users can open them. With a Document Cloud or Creative Cloud subscription, you can use eSign to send a document to others for their digital signatures. Alternatively, you can use digital IDs to sign documents and certify PDF documents. If you want to save security settings for later use, you can create a security policy that stores security settings. In Acrobat Pro, you can also permanently remove sensitive content from your PDF documents using the Redaction feature (see Lesson 5, "Editing Content in PDF Files").

First you'll learn about Protected Mode in Acrobat Reader for Windows, and then you'll work with the security features in Acrobat itself.

Viewing documents in Protected Mode in Reader (Windows only)

As mentioned in Lesson 1, by default, Acrobat Reader DC for Windows opens PDF files in Protected Mode (known as "sandboxing" to IT professionals). In Protected Mode, Reader confines any processes to the application itself, so that potentially malicious PDF files do not have access to your computer and its system files.

To complete this exercise, you must use Acrobat Reader DC for Windows, but Acrobat Reader is not automatically installed with Acrobat. You can download the free installer at get.adobe.com/reader.

1   Open Acrobat Reader DC in Windows.

2   Choose File > Open, and navigate to the Lesson08 folder.

3   Select Travel Guide.pdf, and click Open.

The Travel Guide.pdf file opens in Acrobat Reader. You can access all of the Reader menus and tools. However, the PDF file cannot make calls to your system outside the Reader environment.

4 Choose File > Properties.

5   In the Document Properties dialog box, click the Advanced tab.

6   View the Protected Mode status at the bottom of the dialog box. It's On by default.

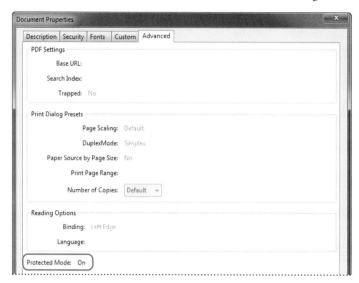

You can always confirm that a document is open in Protected Mode by viewing the Document Properties dialog box.

7   Click OK to close the Document Properties dialog box. Then close the Travel Guide.pdf file, and quit Reader.

Adobe strongly recommends that you use Acrobat Reader in Protected Mode. However, some third-party plug-ins may not work in Protected Mode. If you need to disable Protected Mode, choose Edit > Preferences, select Security (Enhanced) from the list of categories, and deselect Enable Protected Mode At Startup. You'll need to restart Acrobat Reader for the changes to take effect.

About security in Acrobat

You can secure a PDF using any of the following security methods:

• Add passwords and set security options to restrict opening, editing, and printing PDFs.

• Encrypt a document so that only a specified set of users has access to it.

- Save the PDF as a certified document. Certifying a PDF adds a certifying signature (which may be visible or invisible) that lets the document author restrict changes to the document.

- Apply server-based security policies to PDFs (for example, using Adobe LiveCycle Rights Management). Server-based security policies are especially useful if you want others to have access to PDFs for a limited time.

You can also use security envelopes to protect your PDF documents in transit. You'll learn more about those if you choose to complete the "Exploring on your own" section at the end of this lesson.

Viewing security settings

When you open a document that has restricted access or some type of security applied to it, you'll see a Security Settings button (🔒) in the navigation pane to the left of the document window.

1   Start Acrobat. Then choose File > Open, navigate to the Lesson08 folder, and open the Sponsor_secure.pdf file. If the Acrobat Security Settings dialog box appears, click Cancel; if the Trusted Certificates Update dialog box appears, click OK.

2   Notice that "(SECURED)" appears after the filename in the title bar.

3   Open the Comment tool, and notice that the commenting and text markup tools are unavailable.

4 Click the triangle on the left side of the document window to open the navigation pane. Click the Security Settings button (🔒) in the navigation pane to view the security settings. Click the Permission Details link to view more detail.

The Document Properties dialog box lists each action and whether it is allowed. As you read down the list, you'll see that commenting is not allowed, which is why the related tools are dimmed. Signing, printing, editing, and other actions are also not allowed in this document.

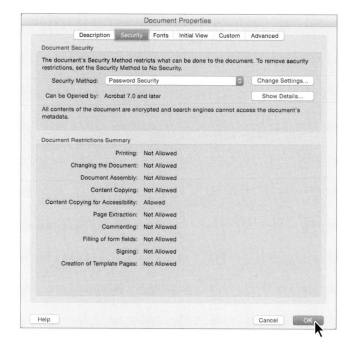

5 When you have finished reviewing the information, click Cancel to close the Document Properties dialog box.

6 Choose File > Close to close the Sponsor_secure.pdf file.

Adding security to PDF files

You can add security to your Adobe PDF files when you first create them, or you can add it later. You can even add security to files that you receive from someone else, unless the creator of the document has limited who can change security settings.

Now, you'll add password protection to limit who can open your document and who can change the security settings.

Adding passwords

You can add two kinds of passwords to protect your Adobe PDF documents. A Document Open password allows only users who enter the password to open the document. A Permissions password allows only users who enter the password to change the permissions for the document, so that they can print or modify the document or perform other changes you've restricted.

You'll add protection to a logo file so that no one can change its contents and so that unauthorized users can't open and use the file.

▶ **Tip:** As long as you have the password, you can open password-protected and encrypted PDF files on tablets and phones using the Acrobat DC mobile app. To learn more, see "Going mobile" on page 6.

1 Choose File > Open, navigate to the Lesson08 folder, and open the Local_Logo.pdf file.

There is no Security Settings button in the navigation pane, because no security has been applied to this document.

2 Choose File > Save As, save the file in the Lesson08 folder, and name the file **Local_Logo1.pdf**.

3 Click Protect in the Tools pane.

4 In the Protect toolbar, click Encrypt, and choose 2 Encrypt With Password. Click Yes when Acrobat asks whether you want to add security to the document.

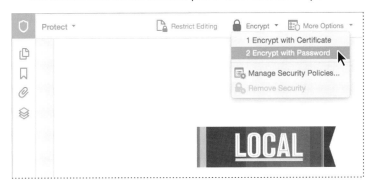

The Password Security – Settings dialog box opens automatically.

5 Select the Require A Password To Open The Document option, and then type **Logo1234;^bg** for the password.

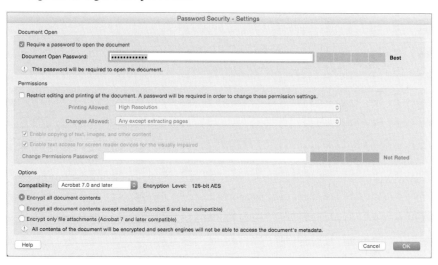

▶ **Tip:** Always record your passwords in a secure location. If you forget your password, you can't recover it from the document. You might also want to store an unprotected copy of the document in a secure location.

Acrobat rates the password's strength. Stronger passwords include both uppercase and lowercase letters, numbers, punctuation marks, and symbols. Longer passwords also tend to be harder to guess. If it's critical that a document remain confidential, use a strong password. You'll share this password with anyone who you want to allow to open the document. Remember that passwords are case-sensitive.

Now you'll add a second password that controls who is allowed to change printing, editing, and security settings for the file.

6 Under Permissions, select Restrict Editing And Printing Of The Document.

7 From the Printing Allowed menu, choose Low Resolution (150 dpi). You can prohibit printing, allow only low-resolution printing, or allow high-resolution printing.

8 From the Changes Allowed menu, choose Commenting, Filling In Form Fields, And Signing Existing Signature Fields to allow users to comment on the logo. You can prohibit all changes, some changes, or only prohibit viewers from extracting pages.

9 In the Change Permissions Password box, type **Logo5678;^bg**. Your open password and permissions password can't be the same.

Next you'll set the compatibility level. The default compatibility level is compatibility with Acrobat 7.0 or later. If you're sure that all your viewers have Acrobat X or later, you should choose Acrobat X And Later, as it provides the strongest protection. If you think that some of your viewers may still be using Acrobat 6.0, select Acrobat 6.0 And Later. Be aware, however, that this setting may use a lower encryption level.

10 Make sure Acrobat 7.0 And Later is selected in the Compatibility menu.

11 Click OK to apply your changes.

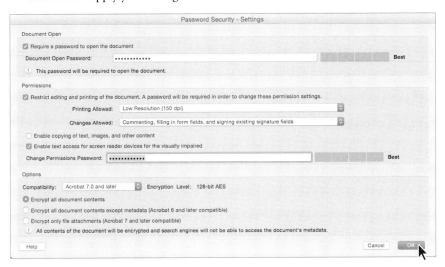

12 In the Confirm Document Open Password dialog box, re-enter the Open Password, **Logo1234;^bg**. Then click OK.

13 Read the alert that warns you that some third-party applications may not honor the security settings in the PDF file, and click OK to clear the alert.

14 In the Confirm Permissions Password dialog box, re-enter the Permissions Password, **Logo5678;^bg**. Then click OK, and click OK again to clear the alert.

The security changes don't take effect until you save the file.

15 Choose File > Save to save the security changes.

16 Click the Security Settings button (🔒) in the navigation pane, and then click the Permission Details link. The limitations you set are in effect.

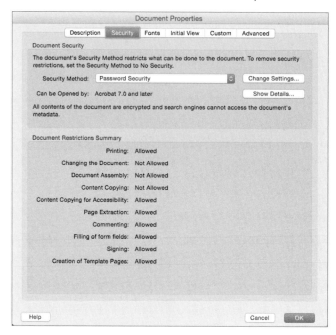

17 Click OK to close the Document Properties dialog box, and then choose File > Close to close the Local_Logo1.pdf file.

Opening password-protected files

Now you'll check the security that you've added to your file.

1 Choose File > Open, and open the Local_Logo1.pdf file in the Lesson08 folder.

Acrobat prompts you to enter the required password to open the file.

2 Enter the password (**Logo1234;^bg**), and click OK.

Notice that "(SECURED)" has been appended to the filename at the top of the application window.

Now you'll test the permissions password.

3   Click the Security Settings button (🔒) in the navigation pane, and click the Permission Details link.

4   In the Document Properties dialog box, try changing the Security Method from Password Security to No Security.

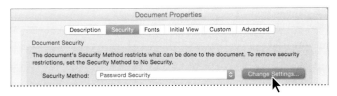

Acrobat prompts you to enter the Permissions password.

5   Enter the password (**Logo5678;^bg**), and click OK; then click OK again to confirm that you want to remove security.

All restrictions are now removed from the file.

6   Click OK to close the Document Properties dialog box.

7   Choose File > Close, and close the file without saving the changes. Because you aren't saving your changes, the passwords remain in effect next time you open the file.

About digital signatures

Signing a document electronically offers several advantages, not least of which is that you can email the signed document rather than having to fax it or send it by courier. Although digitally signing a document doesn't necessarily prevent people from changing the document, it does allow you to track any changes made after the signature is added and revert to the signed version if necessary. (You can prevent users from changing your document by applying appropriate security to the document.)

With an Acrobat Document Cloud subscription or a Creative Cloud subscription, you can use Adobe Document Cloud eSign services (formerly EchoSign) to sign a document or send it out for signatures. ESign makes the process of signing documents electronically fast and simple.

You can also sign a document using certificates: You must obtain a digital ID from a third-party provider or create a digital ID (self-signed digital ID) for yourself in Acrobat. The digital ID contains a private key that is used to add the digital signature and a certificate that you share with those who need to validate your signature.

For information about Adobe security partners that offer third-party digital IDs and other security solutions, visit the Adobe website at www.adobe.com.

Sending a document for others to sign

The easiest way to invite someone else to sign a document electronically is to use Document Cloud eSign Services. You'll prepare a document for eSign, and then send it out for signatures. If you're working with others, you'll send it to a colleague to sign. However, if you're working alone, you'll need to have an alternate email address to use; you can create free email addresses through services such as Gmail and Yahoo Mail.

Preparing the form

If you send a document without preparing it, eSign affixes signature and email fields to the bottom of the document. That may be all you need if, for example, you require only confirmation that someone has read a document. However, most forms require signatures or initials in specific locations, and many require other information as well. You'll prepare a form with standard signature blocks for the client (GlobalCorp) and the vendor (Custom Solutions).

1   In Acrobat, choose File > Open, navigate to the Lesson08 folder, and double-click Statement of Work.pdf.

This document is a contract for services. The signature blocks are on the last page.

2   Click Send For Signature in the Tools pane.

The Send For Signature tool opens.

3   Confirm that Statement of Work.pdf is the selected file.

Your document doesn't include any form fields that eSign will recognize, so you'll need to prepare it before sending it.

4   Click Prepare Form.

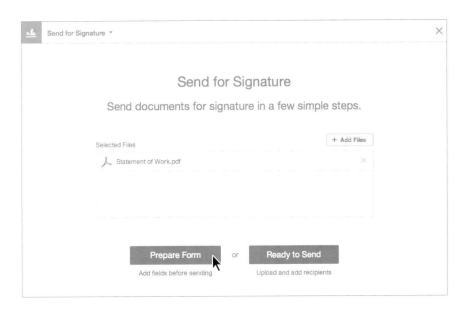

Acrobat opens the Prepare Form tool, and it analyzes the document for existing and likely form fields.

5 Click OK when Acrobat reports that no form fields were found.

6 Go to page 4 in the document to see the signature lines.

7 Select the Add Signature tool (⬚) in the Prepare Form toolbar.

8 Drag a signature form field above the GlobalCorp signature line.

9 Make sure Signer is chosen in the Who Needs To Sign This Field menu.

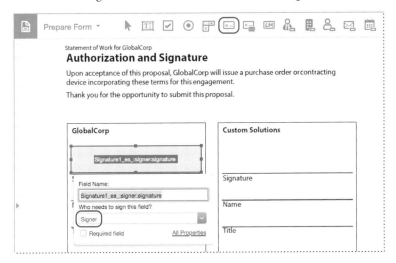

When Sender or one of the Signer options is chosen, the form field becomes an eSign field. If Anyone is chosen in the Who Needs To Sign This Field menu, eSign won't recognize the field.

10 Select the Add Name tool () in the Prepare Form toolbar, drag a field above the GlobalCorp Name line, and make sure Signer is chosen in the Who Needs to Sign This Field menu.

11 Select the Add Title tool () in the Prepare Form toolbar, drag a form field above the GlobalCorp Title line, and make sure Signer is chosen.

When the recipient signs the signature line, eSign will automatically populate the Name field with the signer's name. It will also automatically add the current date to the Date field.

12 Select the Add Date tool () in the Prepare Form toolbar, drag a form field above the GlobalCorp Date line, and make sure Signer is chosen.

You've created the fields for the GlobalCorp signer. Now you'll create the fields for the Custom Solutions representative. Because Custom Solutions is sending the document out, you'll choose Sender from the Who Needs To Sign This Field menu.

13 Select the Add Signature tool, and drag a form field above the Custom Solutions signature line.

14 Choose Sender from the Who Needs To Sign This Field menu. You may need to scroll up to see the option.

15 Use the Add Name, Add Title, and Add Date tools to add the remaining fields, choosing Sender from the Who Needs to Sign This Field menu each time.

Sending the document

All the form fields are in place and recognizable by eSign, so you're ready to send the document. You'll send it to another person to sign for GlobalCorp and to yourself to sign for Custom Solutions. When you enter email addresses in the eSign dialog box, eSign sends the document to each address in the order they're entered. That is, the document is sent to the first person to sign, and when it's been signed, the document—including the first person's signature—is sent to the second person to sign, and so on.

1. Click Send For Signature in the right-hand pane.

2. Confirm that the Statement of Work.pdf document is selected, and then click Ready To Send.

Acrobat uploads the document to the Document Cloud, and then prompts you to add recipients in the order they will sign.

● Note: Acrobat compares the email address you enter with your address book. If it doesn't find the address you enter, it may prompt you to enter an address again. Click the address you already entered to proceed.

3. Enter the email address of the person who should sign the document first, and press Enter or Return. For this exercise, use a colleague's email address or an alternate address you've created. This person will be prompted to sign the fields that are specified for the Signer.

4. Just below the first signer's email address, add the email address from which you're sending the document. This should be the email address associated with your Adobe ID. You'll be prompted to sign the fields specified for the Sender.

5. Customize the message if you want to, and then click Send.

Acrobat uses eSign to send the documents for signature.

6. Click Manage This Document.

Document Cloud eSign Services opens in your default browser. The document you just sent is listed in the Out For Signatures category. After it's been signed, it will be listed in the Signed category instead.

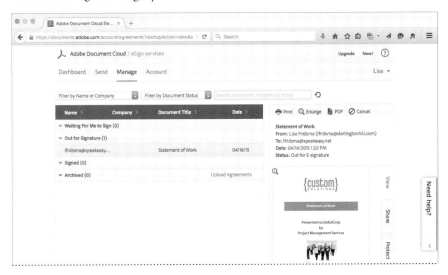

Signing the document

Document Cloud eSign Services sends email to the first address you listed. You'll complete the form for the signer, and then complete it for the sender.

1   Log in to the email account whose address you entered first, the one that would be for the GlobalCorp representative. (If you used a colleague's email address, ask them to access their account.)

2   Open the message with the subject line "Please sign Statement of Work."

3   Read the message, and then click Click Here To Review And Sign Statement of Work.

Adobe Document Cloud eSign Services opens in your default browser.

4 Click the yellow arrow labeled Start to go to the first field that requires your data.

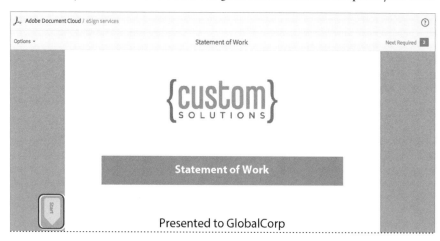

5 Click the GlobalCorp signature field.

A signature dialog box opens.

6 Type your name. If you want it to look like your manual signature, click Draw, and then draw your signature using a stylus, tablet, or touch screen. When you're satisfied with your signature, click Apply.

Whether you select Type or Draw in the signature dialog box, you must type your name so that it is officially recorded in the eSign transaction. Conveniently, eSign automatically fills in the Name field with that information.

7 Type a title in the Title field.

8 Click the Click To Sign button at the bottom of the screen.

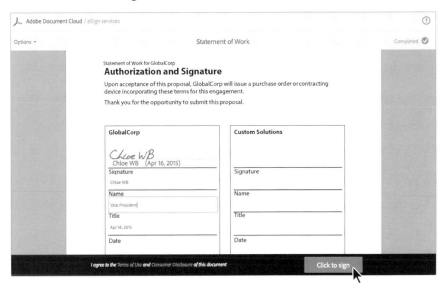

Now that the first person has signed, eSign sends the document to the second email address, which is yours, as the sender.

9 Log in to the email address you used to send the document (the email address associated with your Adobe ID).

10 Open the message with the subject line that reads "Your signature is required on Statement of Work."

The subject line is different from the one in the email message you opened before, because this one is addressing the document's sender.

11 Click the message, and then click Click Here To Review And Sign Statement of Work.

12 Adobe Document Cloud eSign Services opens with the same document. Click the yellow arrow labeled Start.

The GlobalCorp fields are completed. The Custom Solutions fields are now active.

13 Repeat steps 5-8 to sign and complete the Custom Solutions fields and to submit the signed document.

eSign sends messages to all parties informing them that the document has been signed and filed, and it attaches a PDF file of the final signed document to the message.

Using the Fill & Sign tool

With the Fill & Sign tool, you can fill in a form that doesn't include Acrobat form fields, and you can sign anything anywhere. If you're signing official documents, you should probably use eSign or a digital ID to sign your document. But if you're signing a permission slip or other more casual document, the Fill & Sign tool gives you the flexibility to do what you need to do without having to create form fields.

To sign a document using the tool, click Fill & Sign in the Tools pane. Then click Sign in the Fill & Sign toolbar, and choose Add Signature or Add Initials (or choose your name or initials, if Acrobat already has your name and initials stored). Type your name if it's not already there. You can change the style, draw your signature, or even import a scanned image of your signature. Click Apply. The cursor becomes your signature; just click it where you want your signature to appear.

To fill in other fields, select the Add Text tool in the Fill & Sign toolbar, position the cursor on the page, and start typing. Click outside the text box to accept what you've typed.

Creating digital signatures

Document Cloud eSign Services is available only with a Document Cloud or Creative Cloud subscription. If you don't have access to eSign, you can sign PDF files electronically using certificates and digital IDs. Depending on your security and communication needs, you may also prefer to use digital IDs to sign documents, as your digital ID can stamp the time, location, reason for signing, and other information as well as your signature.

For these exercises, you'll use a self-signed digital ID, which is often adequate for signing documents. You can set the appearance of your digital signature, select your preferred signing method, and determine how digital signatures are verified in the Security preferences. You should also set your preferences to optimize Acrobat for validating signatures before you open a signed document.

Adding images to your digital signatures

First you'll add the company logo to your signature block.

1   Choose Edit > Preferences (Windows) or Acrobat > Preferences (Mac OS), and select Signatures from the categories on the left.

2 In the Creation & Appearance area of the dialog box, click More to open the Creation and Appearance Preferences dialog box.

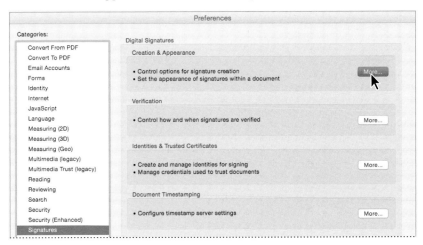

3 In the Appearances section of the dialog box, click New.

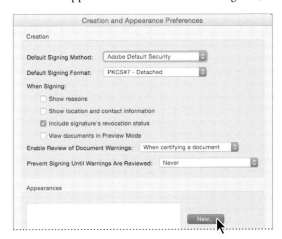

Acrobat opens the Configure Signature Appearance dialog box. This is where you can personalize your digital signature by adding a graphic and specifying which information appears. The Preview pane shows the default digital signature appearance, which is text-based.

First you'll name the appearance of your signature and add a corporate logo to the signature block.

4 In the Title text box, type **Logo**.

When you name a signature appearance, use a name that is easy to associate with the contents of the appearance. You can create several digital signatures for yourself.

5 In the Configure Graphic section of the dialog box, select Imported Graphic, and click File.

6 In the Select Picture dialog box, click Browse, navigate to the Lesson08 folder, and select the Local_Logo.pdf file. Supported file types are listed in the Files Of Type (Windows) or Show (Mac OS) menu. Click Open (Windows) or Select (Mac OS), and then click OK to return to the Configure Signature Appearance dialog box.

Now you'll specify the information to be included in the text block of your signature. You'll include your name, the reason for signing the document, and the date.

7 In the Configure Text area of the Configure Signature Appearance dialog box, select Name, Date, and Reason. Deselect all the other options.

8 When you're happy with the preview of your signature block, click OK.

9   In the When Signing area of the Creation And Appearance Preferences dialog box, select View Documents In Preview Mode and Show Reasons.

10 Make sure that Adobe Default Security is selected from the Default Signing Method menu.

11 Click OK to return to the Preferences dialog box.

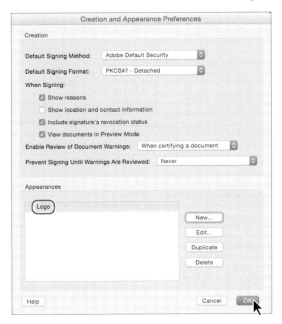

Signing in Preview mode

Use Preview mode when you want to analyze a document for content that may alter the appearance of the document after you sign it. Such content may include transparency, scripts, fonts, and other dynamic content that can alter a document's appearance. Preview mode suppresses this dynamic content, allowing you to view and sign the document in a static and secure state.

When you view a PDF in Preview mode, a document message bar lets you know whether the PDF contains any dynamic content or external dependencies.

To use Preview mode when signing, choose Edit > Preferences (Windows) or Acrobat > Preferences (Mac OS), click Signatures in the list on the left, click More in the Creation And Appearance area, and then select View Documents in Preview Mode under When Signing. Click OK to close out of each preferences dialog box and save the change.

Selecting a verification method

Now you'll specify how Acrobat verifies signatures.

1   In the Verification area of the Preferences dialog box, click More.

In the Signature Verification Preferences dialog box, notice that the Require Certificate Revocation Checking To Succeed Whenever Possible During Signature Verification option is selected. This ensures that certificates are always checked against a list of excluded certificates during validation.

2   Select Use The Document-Specified Method; Prompt If Unavailable (the first option under "When Verifying"). You'll be prompted if you don't have the necessary software when you try to open a document.

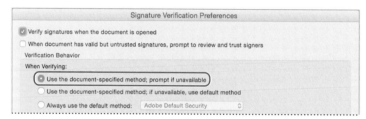

Also in the Verification Behavior area of the dialog box is a pop-up menu enabling you to choose the default method for verifying signatures. The default security method menu is dimmed when the first option is selected. You set the default method to be used when signing and encrypting documents in the Creation And Appearance Preferences dialog box.

In Windows, the Windows Integration area contains options for specifying whether all root certificates in the Windows Certificates can be trusted. We recommend that you leave the default settings in this area.

3   Click OK to close the Signature Verification Preferences dialog box.

Creating digital IDs

A digital ID is similar to a driver's license or passport. It proves your identity to people with whom you communicate electronically. A digital ID usually contains your name and email address, the name of the company that issued your digital ID, a serial number, and an expiration date.

A digital ID lets you create a digital signature or decrypt a PDF document that has been encrypted. You can create more than one digital ID to reflect different roles in your life. For this exercise, you'll create a digital ID for E. Grace, an employee of the fictitious *Local Magazine*.

1   In the Identities & Trusted Certificates area of the Digital Signatures Preferences dialog box, click More.

2   In the Digital ID And Trusted Certificate Settings dialog box, select Digital IDs in the left pane. Then click the Add ID button.

You'll create a self-signed digital ID. With a self-signed ID, you share your signature information with other users using a public certificate. (A certificate is a confirmation of your digital ID and contains information used to protect data.) While this method is adequate for most unofficial exchanges, a more secure approach is to obtain a digital ID from a third-party provider.

3   In the Add Digital ID dialog box, select A New Digital ID I Want To Create Now. Then click Next.

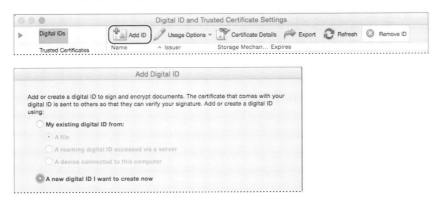

If you're working in Mac OS, skip to step 5. If you're working in Windows, you'll choose where to store your digital ID. The PKCS#12 Digital ID File option stores the information in a file that you can share with others. A Windows Default Certificate Digital ID is stored in the Windows Certificate Store. Because you want to easily share your digital ID with colleagues, you'll use the PKCS#12 option.

4   Make sure that New PKCS#12 Digital File ID is selected, and click Next.

Now you'll enter your personal information.

5   Enter the name you want to appear in the Signatures tab and in any signature field that you complete, and enter a corporate or organization name (if necessary) and an email address. We entered **E. Grace** for the name, **Local Magazine** for the Organization Name, and **local@xyz.net** for the email address. Make sure that you select a Country/Region. We used the default US - United States.

6   Choose 2048-bit RSA from the Key Algorithm menu to set the level of security. 2048-bit RSA offers more security protection than 1024-bit RSA.

You can use a digital ID to control digital signatures, data encryption (security), or both. When you use a digital ID to encrypt a PDF document, you specify a list of recipients from your Trusted Identities, and you define the recipients' level of access to the file—for example, whether the recipients can edit, copy, or print the files. You can also encrypt documents using security policies.

For this exercise, you'll apply the digital ID to digital signatures.

7   From the Use Digital ID For menu, choose Digital Signatures And Data Encryption, and then click Next.

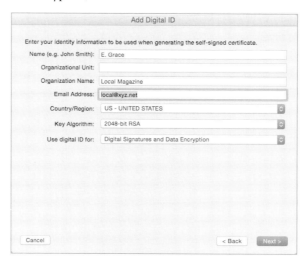

Now you'll save and safeguard your information.

8   Accept the default location for the digital ID file. Then enter **Local1234;^bg** as the password. Re-enter your password to confirm it. Remember that the password is case-sensitive. Be sure to make a note of your password and keep it in a safe place. You cannot use or access your digital ID without this password.

9 Click Finish to save the digital ID file in the Security folder.

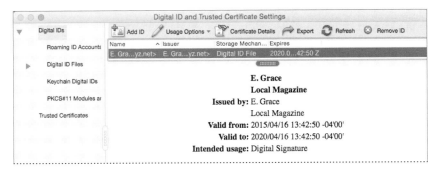

Your new digital ID appears in the Security Settings dialog box.

10 In Windows, select the digital ID to see its details. In Mac OS, double-click it to view the certificate details. When you've finished checking your digital ID, close the dialog box, and then click OK to close the Preferences dialog box.

Sharing certificates with others

Your digital ID includes a certificate that others require to validate your digital signature and to encrypt documents for you. If you know that others will need your certificate, you can send it in advance to avoid delays when exchanging secure documents. Businesses that use certificates to identify participants in secure workflows often store certificates on a directory server that participants can search to expand their list of trusted identities.

If you use a third-party security method, you usually don't need to share your certificate with others. Third-party providers may validate identities using other methods, or these validation methods may be integrated with Acrobat. See the documentation provided by the third-party provider.

When you receive a certificate from someone, their name is added to your list of trusted identities as a contact. Contacts are usually associated with one or more certificates and can be edited, removed, or associated with another certificate. If you trust a contact, you can set your trust settings to trust all digital signatures and certified documents created with their certificate.

You can also import certificates from a certificate store, such as the Windows Certificate Store. A certificate store may contain numerous certificates issued by different certification authorities.

Signing a document digitally with certificates and digital IDs

Because you want the graphic designers to know that the changes to this document are approved and you want them to be sure that no additional changes have been made since the time you approved it, you'll create a visible signature field and sign the document.

First, you'll open the draft of the travel guide document that you'll be signing.

1 Choose File > Open. Navigate to the Lesson08 folder, select Travel Guide.pdf, and click Open. Then choose File > Save As, rename the file **Travel Guide1.pdf**, and save it in the Lesson08 folder.

2 Click Tools to open the Tools Center, and then click Certificates to open the Certificates tool.

3 Click Digitally Sign in the Certificates toolbar.

4 Read the information dialog box that appears, and then click OK.

5 Drag to create a signature field in the area above the map.

Acrobat automatically switches into Preview mode, which analyzes the document for content that may alter the document's appearance and then suppresses that content, enabling you to view and sign the document in a static and secure state.

6 In the preview toolbar across the top of the document window, click Sign Document.

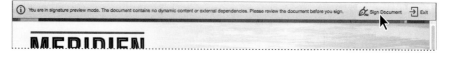

● **Note:** Acrobat switches to Preview mode because you set your preferences to view documents in Preview mode before signing. If you see the Sign Document dialog box instead, choose Edit > Preferences or Acrobat > Preferences, and then select Signatures on the left, and click More in the Creation & Appearance area. Then select View Documents in Preview Mode, and click OK.

7   In the Sign Document dialog box, enter the password associated with the ID in the Sign As text box, **Local1234;^bg**.

8   Choose Logo from the Appearance menu.

9   Choose I Am Approving This Document from the Reason pop-up menu.

10 Click Sign to apply your signature, and click Save to save the signed file. Click Yes or Replace when prompted to replace the original file.

The recipient of the signed document will need your certificate to validate the digital signature.

Modifying signed documents

Now you'll add a comment to the signed document to see how the digital signature information changes. But first you'll look at the Signatures panel to see what a valid signature looks like.

1   Click Signature Panel in the preview toolbar to open the Signatures panel in the navigation pane. If necessary, drag the right margin of the Signatures panel so that you can see all the signature information. Expand the signature line, and expand the Signature Details entry.

Now you'll add a note to the document and see how the addition changes the digital signature.

2 Choose Comment from the Certificates pop-up menu on the left side of the Certificates toolbar.

3 Select the Sticky Note tool (💬) in the Comment toolbar.

4 Click anywhere on the document page to add a note. In the note, type **Good work**.

▶ **Tip:** Use the Signatures panel to review the change history of a document or to track changes when a document is signed using multiple digital signature IDs.

Expand the signature again in the Signatures panel. The signature status has changed with the addition of a note.

Now you'll validate the signature.

5 Right-click (Windows) or Control-click (Mac OS) the signature box in the document pane, and choose Validate Signature.

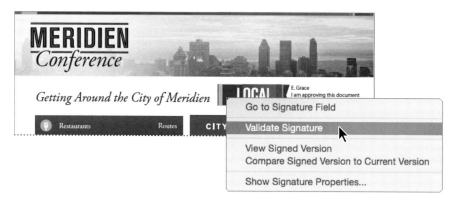

▶ **Tip:** Right-click (Windows) or Control-click (Mac OS) the signature box in the document pane, and choose Show Signature Properties to resolve any issues with the signature.

6 The alert box explains that although the signature is valid, a change has been made. Click Close to close the warning box.

7   Right-click (Windows) or Control-click (Mac OS) the signature box in the document pane, and choose View Signed Version.

The View Signed Version option recovers the unchanged file. If a document has signatures on multiple versions of the document, for example, you can view any previously signed version of the document by selecting the signature in the Signatures panel and then choosing View Signed Version from the options menu.

8   Close both open PDF files. You do not need to save your work.

Certifying PDF files

You can also certify the contents of a PDF document. Certifying a document rather than signing it is useful if you want the user to be able to make approved changes to a document. When you certify a document and a user makes approved changes, the certification is still valid. You can certify forms, for example, to guarantee that the content is valid when the user receives the form. As the creator of the form, you can specify what tasks the user can perform. For example, you can specify that readers can fill in the form fields without invalidating the document. However, if a user tries to add or remove a form field or a page, the certification will be invalidated.

Now you'll certify a form to be sent to sponsors of a conference. By certifying the form, you ensure that the sponsors fill out the form as you designed it, with no additions or deletions to the form fields.

1   Choose File > Open, navigate to the Lesson08 folder, and open the Sponsor.pdf file.

For information on the Forms message bar, see Lesson 10, "Working with Forms in Acrobat."

2   Choose File > Properties, and click the Security tab.

The information in the Document Properties dialog box shows that no security and no restrictions have been applied to the document.

3   Click Cancel to close the Document Properties dialog box without making any changes.

4   Click Tools, and then click the Certificates tool to open it.

5   Click Certify (Visible Signature) in the Certificates toolbar.

6   In the dialog box that appears, click Drag New Signature Rectangle. Then click
    OK in the Save As Certified Document dialog box.

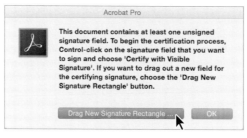

You'll use the digital ID that you created earlier in the lesson to certify the file.

7   Drag anywhere in the document to create a signature field. We created a signature
    field in the upper left corner, below the Local logo.

8   Click the Sign Document button on the document message bar.

9   In the Certify Document dialog box, if you have created more than one digital
    ID, select the digital ID to use. We selected E. Grace.

10 Enter the password, **Local1234;^bg**.

11 Choose Logo from the Appearance pop-up menu.

12 From the Reason menu, choose I Attest To The Accuracy And Integrity
    Of This Document.

13 From the Permitted Actions After Certifying menu, choose Annotations,
    Form Fill-In, And Digital Signatures.

14 Click Sign to complete the certification process.

15 Save your file as **Sponsor_Cert.pdf**.

16 Click the Signatures button (✑) in the navigation pane to open the Signatures panel, and review which actions the certification allows. You may need to expand the certification entry.

▶ **Tip:** Whenever you open a certified document, you'll see a Certification icon at the left of the message bar. You can click this icon at any time to see certification information for the document.

17 When you've finished reviewing the certification information, close the Signatures panel.

Signing certified documents

Now you'll sign the document that you just certified to verify that filling in a signature field doesn't invalidate the certification.

1 Go to page 2 in the document.

2 With the Hand tool selected, click in the Local Signature box at the bottom of the document. Then click the Sign Document button on the document message bar.

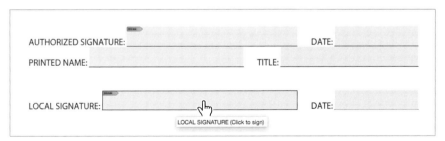

The Sign Document dialog box opens.

3 In the dialog box, if you have more than one digital ID defined, select your digital ID. We selected E. Grace.

4 Enter the password, **Local1234;^bg**.

5 Leave the other values, click Sign, and save the file in the Lesson08 folder using the same filename. Click Yes or Replace to replace the original file.

6 Click the Signatures button in the navigation pane, and expand the certification entry marked with the ribbon icon.

Notice that the certification is still valid even though a signature has been added.

7 Choose File > Close.

Securing PDFs in FIPS mode (Windows)

Acrobat and Reader provide FIPS mode to restrict data protection to Federal Information Processing Standard (FIPS) 140-2 approved algorithms using the RSA BSAFE Crypto-C 2.1 encryption module.

The following options are not available in FIPS mode:

- **Applying password-based security policies to documents**—You can use public key certificates or Adobe LiveCycle Rights Management to secure the document, but you cannot use password encryption to secure the document.

- **Creating self-signed certificates**—In FIPS mode, you cannot create self-signed certificates. You can open and view documents that are protected with non-FIPS compliant algorithms, but you cannot save any changes to the document using password security. To apply security policies to the document, use either public key certificates or LiveCycle Rights Management.

Review questions

1 What is Document Cloud eSign Services?

2 Where do you change the appearance of your digital signature if you're using a certificate?

3 Why would you want to apply password protection to a PDF file?

4 Why would you apply permissions protection to a PDF file?

Review answers

1 Document Cloud eSign Services is an electronic signature service that makes it easier for individuals and businesses to sign documents quickly and securely. If you have a Document Cloud or Creative Cloud subscription, you can use eSign to send unlimited documents for signatures, and to track and manage those documents.

2 You change the appearance of your digital signature in the Configure Signature Appearance dialog box. You can access this dialog box from the Security Preferences dialog box. You can also change the appearance of your digital signature in the Sign Document dialog box during the signing process.

3 If you have a confidential document that you don't want others to read, you can apply password protection. Only users with whom you share your password will be able to open the document.

4 Permissions protection limits how a user can use or reuse the contents of your Adobe PDF file. For example, you can specify that users cannot print the contents of your file, or copy and paste the contents of your file. Permissions protection allows you to share the content of your file without losing control over how it is used.

9 USING ACROBAT IN A REVIEW CYCLE

Lesson overview

In this lesson, you'll do the following:

- Discover multiple ways to use Acrobat in a document review process.

- Annotate a PDF file with the Acrobat commenting and markup tools.

- View, reply to, search, and summarize document comments.

- Import comments.

- Initiate an email-based review.

 This lesson will take approximately 60 minutes to complete. Copy the Lesson09 folder onto your hard drive if you haven't already done so.

Robust commenting tools and collaboration features in Acrobat keep review cycles efficient and make it easy for stakeholders to give feedback.

About the review process

There are several ways to use Acrobat in a document review process. No matter which method you use, the workflow contains some core elements: the review initiator invites participants and makes the document available to them, reviewers comment, and the initiator gathers and works with those comments.

You can share any PDF document by email, on a network server, or on a website, and ask individuals to comment on it using Acrobat Reader, Acrobat Standard, or Acrobat Pro. If you post the document or email it manually, you'll need to keep track of returned comments and merge them as you receive them. If you're requesting feedback from only one or two other people, this might be the most efficient way for you to work. For most reviews, however, you can gather comments more efficiently using a shared review process. Additionally, in a shared review, reviewers can see and respond to each others' comments.

When you initiate an email-based review in Acrobat, a wizard helps you send the PDF file as an email attachment, track responses, and manage the comments you receive. Anyone with Acrobat or Reader can add comments to the PDF file.

When you initiate a shared review in Acrobat, a wizard helps you post the PDF file to a network folder, WebDAV folder, or SharePoint workspace. Through the wizard, you email invitations to reviewers, who then access the shared document, add comments, and read others' comments using Acrobat or Reader. You can set a deadline for the review, after which no reviewers can publish additional comments.

Getting started

In this lesson, you'll add comments to a PDF document, view and manage comments, and initiate an email-based review. By definition, collaboration requires you to work with other people. Therefore, many of the exercises in this lesson will be more meaningful if you work through them with one or more colleagues or friends. However, if you are working independently, you can complete the exercises using alternative email addresses, available through web services such as Gmail and Yahoo Mail. (See the legal agreements on their websites for information on how you may use their email accounts.)

First, open the document you'll work with.

1   In Acrobat, choose File > Open.

2   Navigate to the Lesson09 folder, and double-click the Profile.pdf file.

3   Click Comment in the Tools pane.

Adding comments to a PDF document

You can add comments to any PDF file, unless security has been applied to the document to prohibit commenting. In most cases, you'll use the commenting features to provide feedback to a document's author, but you may also find them useful to write notes to yourself as you're reading documents. Acrobat includes several commenting tools. You'll recognize some of them from the physical world. For example, the Sticky Note and Highlight Text tools are electronic versions of physical tools you may have on your desk.

In this exercise, you'll use some of the commenting tools to provide feedback on an article about a fashion designer.

▶ **Tip:** You can add comments to a PDF file on a tablet or phone using the Acrobat DC mobile app. To learn more, see "Going mobile" on page 6.

About the commenting tools

Acrobat provides several commenting and markup tools, designed for different commenting tasks. Most comments include two parts: the markup or icon that appears on the page, and a text message that appears in a pop-up note when you select the comment. Markup and icon tools are available in the Comment toolbar when the Comment tool is open. For detailed information about using each tool, see Adobe Acrobat DC Help.

- **Sticky Note tool** (🗨) – Create sticky notes, just as you would in the physical world. Click wherever you want the note to appear. Sticky notes are useful when you want to make overall comments about a document or a section of a document, rather than commenting on a particular phrase or sentence.

- **Highlight Text tool** (✐) – Highlight text. To add a comment, double-click the highlight on the page.

- **Underline tool** (T̲) – Indicate which text should be underlined.

- **Add Note To Text tool** (T̊) – Highlight text, and add a note regarding the highlighted content.

- **Strikethrough tool** (T̶) – Indicate which text should be deleted.

- **Replace Text tool** (T̲ₐ) – Indicate which text should be removed, and type the text that should replace it.

- **Insert Text tool** (Tₐ) – Add text at the insertion point. As with all the text commenting tools, your comments don't affect the text in the PDF document, but they make your intention clear.

- **Text Correction Markup tool** (T☆) – Mark up text for insertion, replacement, or deletion. This tool combines the Insert Text, Replace Text, and Strikethrough tools.

- **Add Text tool** (T) – Type text that appears directly on the page; like other comments, it won't change the document itself. You can move it, but unlike a pop-up note, you can't hide it.

- **Text Box tool** (🔲) – Create a box that contains text, positioned anywhere on the page, and at any size. It remains visible on the page.

- **Pencil tool** (✐) – Draw freeform lines and shapes on the page.

- **Eraser tool** (⬦) – Erase lines you've drawn.

▶ **Tip:** To create a custom stamp, click the Stamp tool and choose Custom Stamps > Create. Then select the image file you want to use.

- **Stamp tool** (🖳) – Use a virtual rubber stamp to approve a document, mark it confidential, or perform several other common stamping tasks. You can also create custom stamps for your own purposes.

- **Attach File tool** (📎) – Attach a file, in any format, to the PDF document.

- **Record Audio tool** (🎤) – Clarify your feedback aurally by using an audio recording. To record audio, you must have a built-in or removable microphone on your system.

- **Drawing tools** (✏️) – Use the drawing tools to emphasize areas on the page or communicate your thoughts visually, especially when reviewing graphical documents. You can use the **Line** (—), **Arrow** (⇨), **Rectangle** (☐), **Oval** (○), **Text callout** (☐'), **Polygon** (○), **Cloud** (○), and **Connected Lines** (○) tools. You can also expand the drawing tools to include them on the Comment toolbar.

● **Note:** Text callouts let you specify the area you're commenting on without obscuring it. Callout markups have three parts: a text box, a knee line, and an endpoint line. Drag handles to resize each part and position it exactly where you want it.

Commenting in Acrobat Reader

Acrobat Reader DC and Reader XI include all the commenting and markup tools. In Reader X, users had access to the Sticky Note and Highlight Text tools, but other tools were available only if they had been extended for the document in Acrobat.

Adding sticky notes

You can attach a sticky note anywhere in a document. Because notes can easily be moved, they are best suited to comments about the overall content or layout of a document, rather than to specific phrasing. You'll add a sticky note on the first page of this document.

1 Select the Sticky Note tool in the Comment toolbar.

2 Click anywhere on the page.

A sticky note opens. The name in the Identity panel of the Acrobat Preferences dialog box automatically appears on the note, as well as the date and time.

3 Type **Looks good so far. I'll look again when it's finished.**

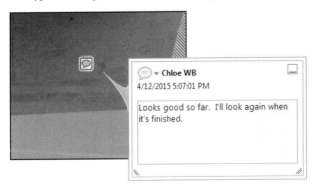

4 Click the arrow that appears before the name in the Sticky Note dialog box, and choose Properties from the pop-up menu.

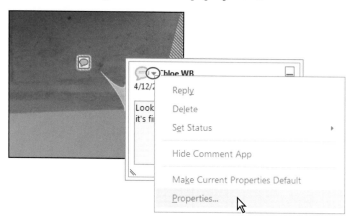

5 Click the Appearance tab, and then click the Color swatch.

6 Select a blue swatch. The sticky note changes color automatically.

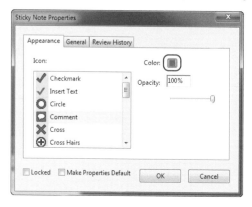

7 Click the General tab and then, in the Author box, type **Reviewer A**.

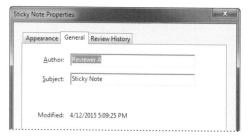

You can change the name attached to a comment. You may want to do that, for example, if you are using someone else's computer.

8 Click OK.

The contents of your note are displayed in the right-hand pane. The blue sticky note is closed on the page. To reopen it, just double-click the sticky note icon.

Emphasizing text

Use the Highlight Text tool to emphasize specific text in a document. After highlighting the text, you can also add a message. You'll make a comment using the Highlight Text tool in this document.

1   Scroll to page 3 in the document.

2   Select the Highlight Text tool (⌀) in the Comment toolbar.

3   Drag the pointer over "ital" at the bottom of the second paragraph on the page. The text is highlighted in yellow.

4   Double-click the highlighted text. A comment message box opens.

5   Type **bad line break**.

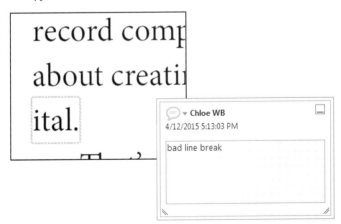

6   Click the close button (⌑) in the upper right corner of the comment box to close it. Alternatively, you can press the Esc key to close the comment box.

Marking text edits

You can clearly communicate which text should be deleted, inserted, or replaced using the text-editing tools. You'll suggest some text changes to the profile article.

1 Scroll to page 2 of the document.

2 Select the Replace Text tool (T̲ₐ) in the Comment toolbar.

3 Select the words "Self reinvention" at the top of the page.

4 Type **Self-reinvention** to replace it.

A comment box appears with the text "Self-reinvention" in it, and the original text is crossed out. An insertion point appears in the original text.

5 Click the close button in the comment box.

6 Select the Insert Text tool (Tₐ) in the Comment toolbar. Then click an insertion point after "dress" in the last paragraph in the right column.

7 Type a dash (-) to indicate that a hyphen should be inserted in the text.

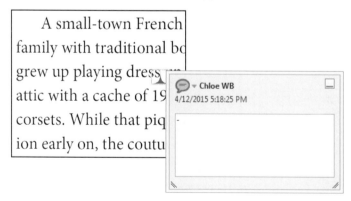

The comment box opens with "-" in it. An insertion point icon appears in the original text.

8 Click the close button in the comment box.

9 Select the Strikethrough tool (T̶) in the Comment toolbar.

10 Select the words "Which raises a really good question:" in the second paragraph in the right column.

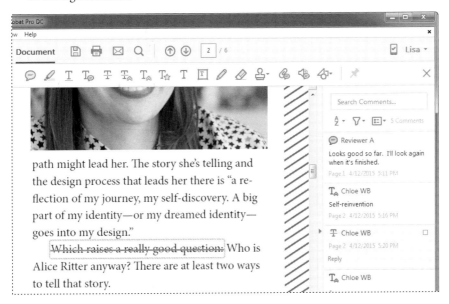

A red line appears through the text, indicating deletion.

11 Go to page 5, select the Text Correction Markup tool (T☆), and click OK in the informational dialog box that appears.

12 Select the word "Emmanuelle" at the bottom of the left column, and then type **"Emmanuelle"** to indicate that quotation marks should be added to the text.

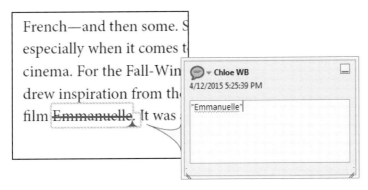

The Text Correction Markup tool gives you flexibility. It's handy to use if you're not sure which kind of correction you're going to make.

13 Choose File > Save As. Save the file in the Lesson09 folder, and name the file **Profile_review.pdf**.

Working with comments

You can view comments on the page, in a list, or in a summary. You can import, export, search, and print comments. You can also reply to comments if you're participating in a shared review or will be returning the PDF file to a reviewer in an email-based review. In this exercise, you'll import comments from reviewers, sort comments, show and hide comments, search for comments, and change their status.

Importing comments

If you use a managed shared review process, comments are imported automatically. However, if you're using an email-based review process or collecting comments informally, you can import comments manually. You'll import comments from three reviewers into the draft of the designer profile.

1 With the Profile_review.pdf file open, notice the comments in the right-hand pane. The only comments in the document are the ones you added.

2 From the options menu (▤) in the right-hand pane, choose Import Data File.

3 Navigate to the Lesson09/Comments folder.

4 Shift-click to select the following files:

- Profile_Art_Director.pdf
- Profile_Linda.pdf
- Profile_Stan.fdf

● **Note:** If you see a message that comments were made on a different version of the document, click OK or Yes to import them anyway.

5 Click Open (Windows) or Select (Mac OS).

Two of the documents are PDF files with comments included; the FDF file is a data file that contains comments that a reviewer exported.

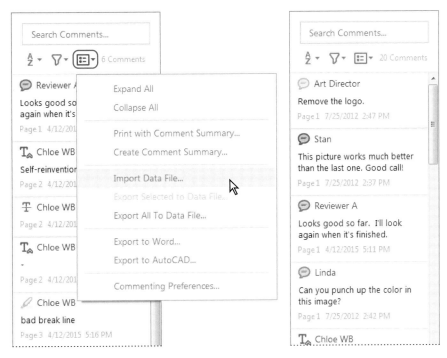

Acrobat imports the comments and displays them in the comments list.

Viewing comments

The comments list appears in the right-hand pane when you import comments. The comments list includes every comment in the document, with the comment author's name, the type of comment, and the comment itself.

1   Scroll through the comments list. By default, comments are listed in the order they appear in the document.

2   Above the comments list, click the Sort Comments button (A/Z), and then choose Author.

Acrobat rearranges the comments so that they are categorized by author name, with authors appearing in alphabetical order.

▶ **Tip:** As a reviewer, you can export comments to a data file (named with an .fdf extension) to reduce file size, especially if you're submitting comments by email. To export comments, choose Export All To Data File or Export Selected To Data File from the options menu in the right-hand pane when the Comment tool is open.

3 Click the Art Director's comment about a hyphen. When you click it, Acrobat moves the page to the comment location so that you can see it in context.

4 Click the check box next to the comment so that it has a check mark in it.

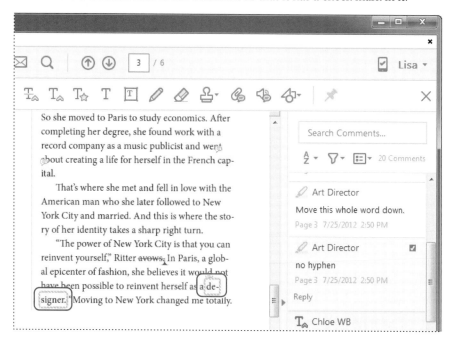

You can add check marks to indicate that you've read a comment, replied to it, discussed it with someone, or anything else that is meaningful to you.

5 Click the Filter Comments button (▽) above the comments list, and choose Checked > Unchecked.

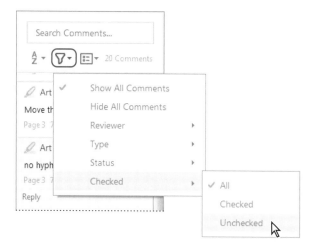

The comment you checked is no longer listed, but it remains in the document. You can use the filter options to declutter the comments list and focus on the comments you want to work with, whether you want to see only text edits, comments by a particular reviewer, or comments that meet other criteria.

6 Click the Filter Comments button again, and choose Show All Comments.

All the comments are listed again.

7 Above the comments list, type **logo** in the Search box.

Only one comment appears in the list, the only comment that includes the word "logo." You can use the Search box to search for any text in comments.

8 Select the comment, and then click Reply beneath the comment. A reply box opens in the comments list, with your name next to it.

9 Type **Legal says the logo is required, per Janet**.

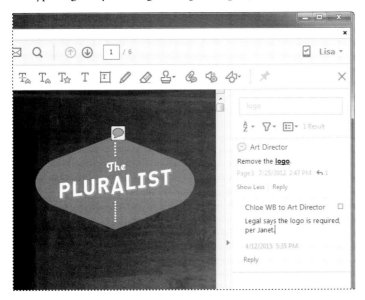

● **Note:** The reviewer will see your reply only if you are using a shared review process or if you email a saved copy of the PDF file to the reviewer.

10 With the last comment still selected, right-click or Control-click the comment, and choose Set Status > Completed.

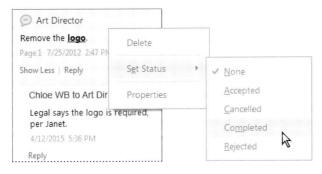

You can set the status of each comment for your own records and to show reviewers how their comments were handled.

11 Close the document; save the changes if you like.

Summarizing comments

You can create a summary of comments, either as a list of only the comments, or as the document with comments referenced. From the options menu above the comments list, choose Create Comment Summary. In the Create Comment Summary dialog box, select the layout and other options for your summary. Then click Create Comment Summary. Acrobat creates and opens a separate PDF file with the comments summary layout you selected. You can view the summary onscreen or print it if you prefer to work with paper.

Initiating an email-based review

In an email-based review, you use Acrobat to distribute the document for review, track reviewers' participation, and consolidate review comments. You'll need to invite at least one other person to participate. If you are working on your own, you may want to create an alternative email address using a free web service such as Gmail or Yahoo Mail.

Inviting reviewers

You'll use a wizard to invite reviewers to participate in an email-based review of a document.

1 Decide who you will invite to participate in the review, and make sure you have their email addresses. If you are working on this lesson alone, create an alternative email address that you can send an invitation to.

2 Choose File > Open.

3   Navigate to the Lesson09 folder, and double-click the Registration.pdf file.

4   Click Tools to open the Tools Center, and then click Send For Comments to open it.

5   Click Send For Comments By Email in the Send For Comments toolbar.

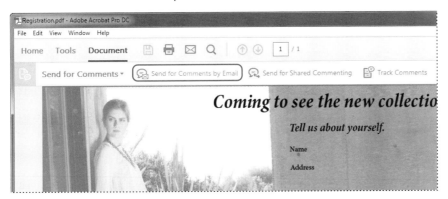

Acrobat prompts you to enter identity information if it doesn't already have it.

6   Enter your name, company name, title, and email address if prompted, and then click Complete.

Identity information lets reviewers know who you are when they receive your invitation to review the document. When Acrobat has your identity information, it opens the Send For Comments By Email wizard.

7   In the Getting Started dialog box, read the informational text, make sure Registration.pdf is chosen as the document for review, and then click Next.

8   In the Invite Reviewers dialog box, enter email addresses for the people you want to invite to review the document. You can use your address book or type addresses directly, separating them with semicolons. Then click Next.

● **Note:** If you are prompted for your Adobe ID and password, enter them.

9   In the Preview Invitation dialog box, customize the message that will be sent to participants, or accept the default message. The default message provides instructions for participating in the review.

10 Click Send Invitation.

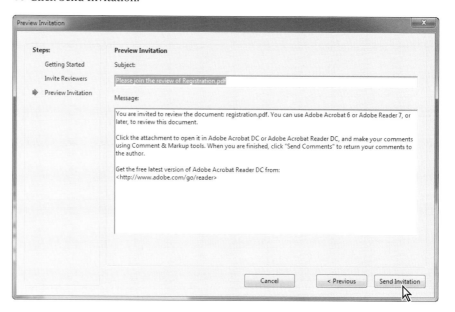

11 In the Send Email dialog box, specify whether to use your defaul mail application or a webmail service. If you use a webmail service, such as Gmail or Yahoo Mail, choose it from the pop-up menu, and then add account information as required. Click Continue.

12 If prompted, provide permission for Acrobat to access the webmail service.

● **Note:** If you see a message warning you that the email addresses are not in your address book, click OK.

13 Click OK in the Outgoing Message Notification dialog box.

14 If necessary, open your default email application and send the message. Some email applications will not automatically send messages, as a security measure.

Acrobat sends invitation email messages with a link to the document on Document Cloud. Acrobat saves your document to Document Cloud and to your local hard drive. Depending on your email application and security settings, your email application may open.

15 Close the document.

Participating in an email-based review

You or your colleague will participate in the email-based review, adding comments about the document.

1   If you're working alone, open the email invitation you sent to an alternative email address. If you're working with a colleague or friend, ask them to open the email invitation you sent and to follow the steps below.

2   Open the attached PDF file in Acrobat.

3   Add several comments to the PDF file using the commenting tools.

4   Click Send Comments in the message bar.

5   In the Send Comments dialog box, confirm the email address of the person who should receive the comments, and then customize the subject and message if you like. Click Send.

6   Choose whether to use the default email application or a webmail application. If you are using a webmail application, select it and provide any required information and permissions. Depending on your default email application's security features, you may also need to manually send the message.

● **Note:** If you open the attached PDF file on the same computer you sent it from, Acrobat recognizes the document and offers to merge any previous comments with it. Click Merge Comments to view the Comment toolbar, make comments, and then choose File > Send File > Attach to Email, and send the PDF file to yourself.

Tracking review comments

You can keep track of reviewers' comments and reply to comments yourself from within Acrobat. You'll open the review PDF file and merge its comments with your copy of the document.

1   Open the email that contains the PDF file with review comments, and then open the attachment.

Acrobat displays a Merge Comments? dialog box.

2   Click Yes in the Merge Comments? dialog box, and then click OK to close the informational dialog box.

The comments you made appear in the comments list in the right-hand pane.

3   Close the Comment tool.

4   Click Tools, and then open the Send For Comments tool.

5   Click Track Comments in the Send For Comments toolbar.

Tip: In Acrobat Pro, you can see what's changed between two versions of a PDF document. Choose View > Compare Documents, specify the document, and select the type of document. Acrobat highlights changes.

Tracker opens.

6 In the left pane of the Tracker dialog box, click Registration under Reviews > Sent. Tracker displays information about the file you sent for review.

Tracker lists the initiator of the review (you) and the email addresses of the people you invited to review the document. Because it cannot monitor your email, it does not list whether individual reviewers have commented or replied. However, you can keep track of when you sent the files for review and who you sent them to. You can also email all reviewers or add reviewers.

7 Close Tracker, and then close the document.

Starting a shared review

In a shared review, all participants can view and respond to each others' comments. Using a shared review is an effective way to let reviewers resolve conflicting opinions, identify areas for research, and develop creative solutions during the review process. You can host a shared review on a network folder, WebDAV folder, or SharePoint workspace.

To start a shared review, open the Send For Comments tool, and then click Send For Shared Commenting in the Send For Comments toolbar. Follow the steps in the wizard to share the file on your server and invite reviewers.

You can set a deadline for review comments in a shared review; after the deadline, commenting tools will no longer be available when reviewers open the document.

Review questions

1 How do you add comments to a PDF document?

2 How can you consolidate comments made by several reviewers?

3 What is the difference between an email-based review process and a shared review process?

Review answers

1 You can add comments to a PDF using any of the commenting and markup tools in Acrobat. Open the Comment tool to see all the tools available in the Comment toolbar. To use a tool, select it, click on the page, and then select the text you want to edit, or draw your markup.

2 To consolidate review comments, open the original PDF file that you sent out for review, and then choose Import Data File from the Comments List panel menu. Select the PDF or FDF files that reviewers returned to you, and click Select. Acrobat imports all the comments into the original document.

3 In an email-based review process, each reviewer receives the PDF document through email, makes comments, and returns the PDF document through email; reviewers do not see each others' comments.

In a shared review process, you post the PDF document to a central server or folder, and then invite reviewers to make their comments. When reviewers publish comments, they can be seen by all other reviewers, so everyone can respond to each other. You can also enforce a deadline more easily with a shared review process, as commenting tools are no longer available to reviewers after the deadline.

10 WORKING WITH FORMS IN ACROBAT

Lesson overview

In this lesson, you'll do the following:

- Create an interactive PDF form.

- Add form fields, including text boxes, radio buttons, and action buttons.

- Distribute a form.

- Track a form to determine its status.

- Learn how to collect and compile form data.

- Validate and calculate form data.

 This lesson will take approximately 45 minutes to complete. Copy the Lesson10 folder onto your hard drive if you haven't already done so.

Aquo Energy Drinks, Ltd.
345 Park Avenue, San Jose, California 95110-2704   phone 555.555.6000   fax 555.555.6001   www.aquo-drinks.com

FEEDBACK

Thank you for working with Aquo's IT team to update your software.
We'd love to hear how we did the job for you.

1. What software did you have updated? (check all that apply)
☐ word processor
☐ spreadsheet
☐ project planning software
☐ email client
☐ operating system

2. Did the technician show up on time for your appointment?
◯ Yes   ◯ No

3. How would you rate the AQUO IT team's performance on the following?
(1 is 'terrible', 3 is 'adequate', 5 is 'fantastic')
Professionalism:
☐ 1   ☐ 2   ☐ 3   ☐ 4   ☐ 5
Technical Expertise:
☐ 1   ☐ 2   ☐ 3   ☐ 4   ☐ 5
Speed/Efficiency of work:
☐ 1   ☐ 2   ☐ 3   ☐ 4   ☐ 5
Ability to communicate process and next steps:
☐ 1   ☐ 2   ☐ 3   ☐ 4   ☐ 5
Ease of setting up your appointment:
☐ 1   ☐ 2   ☐ 3   ☐ 4   ☐ 5

4. How was the support/training documentation that the technician provided for your new software?
☐ There's way too much content
☐ It's exactly the right amount of content
☐ It's much too short—I want more
☐ I did not receive any documentation

You can convert any Acrobat document, including a scanned paper file, into an interactive form for online distribution, tracking, and collection.

Getting started

In this lesson, you'll prepare a feedback form for the IT department of a fictitious beverage manufacturing company. You'll convert an existing PDF document into an interactive form, and use the form tools in Acrobat to add form fields that users can complete online. Then you'll distribute the form, track it, collect the responses, and analyze the data, all using tools within Acrobat.

Converting PDF files to interactive PDF forms

With Acrobat, you can create interactive PDF forms from documents you've created in other applications, such as Microsoft Word or Adobe InDesign, or scanned in from existing paper forms. You will start by opening a flat form that has already been converted to PDF. You will then use the forms tools to convert it to an interactive form.

1   Start Acrobat. Then choose File > Open, and navigate to the Lesson10 folder. Open the Feedback.pdf file.

2   Click Prepare Form in the Tools pane.

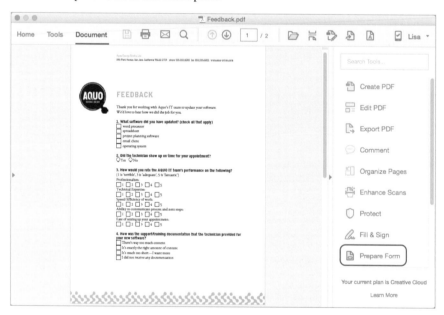

The PDF document contains the text for the form, but Acrobat doesn't recognize any form fields in the document yet.

3 Make sure the Feedback.pdf file is selected, and that form field auto detection is on. Then click Start. (If form field auto detection is off, click Change, and then turn it on.)

Acrobat analyzes the document and adds interactive form fields. You can inspect the document to ensure that Acrobat added form fields appropriately, and you can add fields manually where necessary.

Acrobat lists the form fields it added in the Fields panel on the right. The Prepare Form toolbar and the right-hand pane display the tools available for editing forms.

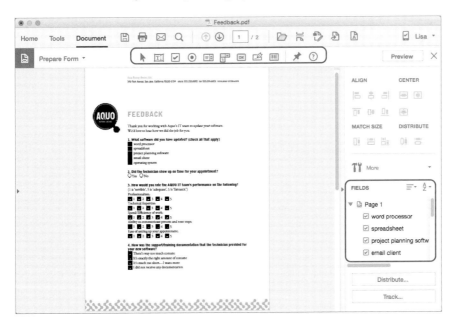

Adding form fields

● **Note:** If a document has been password-protected to prevent editing, you must know the password to add or edit fields.

You can use the form tools in Acrobat to add form fields to any document. Each form field has a name, which should be unique and descriptive; you'll use this name when you collect and analyze data, but it does not appear on the form the user sees. You can add tool tips and labels to help users understand how to complete form fields.

Adding a text field

Acrobat found most of the form fields in the document, but it missed a couple of fields on the second page. You'll add a text field for an email address. Text fields enable users to enter information, such as their name or telephone number, on a form.

1   Scroll to the second page of the PDF file.

2   Select the Text Field tool in the Prepare Form toolbar. Your pointer becomes a text box.

▶ **Tip:** To position fields exactly where you want them, use the Position tab in the field's Properties dialog box. To change the width, height, or position of multiple fields at once, select them, and make the change in the Properties dialog box for one of the fields. You can also lock the width and height of a field so you don't accidentally resize it as you move it.

3   Click to the right of "Email address (optional):" to place the text field.

4   Type **email address** in the Field Name box. Do not select Required Field, because this is an optional field.

5   Drag the right edge of the text field to make it longer.

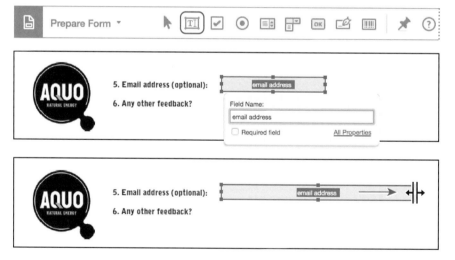

Adding a multiline text field

The next field is for additional feedback. Someone completing the form could type just a few words or a complete paragraph. You'll create a text field that supports multiple lines.

1 Select the Text Field tool in the Prepare Form toolbar.

2 Click below "6. Any other feedback?" to add a text field.

3 Type **other feedback** in the Field Name box. This is another optional field, so do not select Required Field.

4 Drag the lower right blue handle to increase the size of the box so that it could contain multiple lines of text.

5 Double-click the text field to edit its properties.

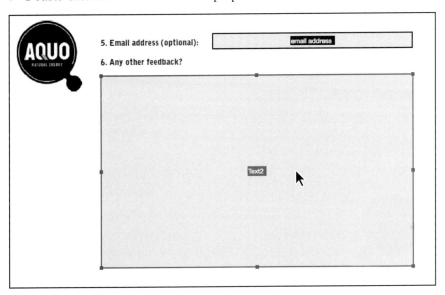

6 In the Text Field Properties dialog box, click the Options tab.

7 Select Multi-line and Scroll Long Text.

8 Select Limit Of _ Characters, and type **750** for the limit.

9 Click Close.

10 Click Preview in the Prepare Form toolbar.

In Preview mode, form fields appear as they will to the person completing the form.

Adding radio buttons

The second question on the feedback form requires a yes-or-no answer. You'll create radio buttons for that question. Radio buttons let the user select one—and only one—option from a set of options.

1   If you're in Preview mode, click Edit in the Prepare Form toolbar to return to Form Editing mode.

2   Go to page 1 of the form.

3   Select the Radio Button tool in the Prepare Form toolbar.

4   Click the circle next to the word "Yes" after question 2.

5   Select Required Field.

6   Type **Yes** in the Radio Button Choice box.

7   Type **on time** in the Group Name box.

8   Click Add Another Button at the bottom of the dialog box. Your pointer becomes a box again.

● **Note:** All radio buttons in a set need to have the same group name.

9   Click the circle next to "No."

10 Type **No** in the Radio Button Choice box, and confirm that the group name is "on time" and that Required Field is selected. Then click outside the dialog box to close it.

11 Click Preview in the Prepare Form toolbar. For the second question, click Yes, and then click No. Notice that you can select only one radio button at a time.

2. Did the technician show up on time
◯ Yes ◉ No

Specifying an answer format

You can use special formatting to restrict the type of data that is entered into a text field, or to automatically convert data into a specific format. For example, you can set a zip code field to accept only numbers, or a date field to accept only a specific date format. And you can restrict numerical entries to numbers within a certain range.

To restrict the format for a text field, open its properties. Click the Format tab, select the format category, and then select the appropriate option for your field.

Adding an action button

Buttons let users perform an action, such as playing a movie file, going to a different page, or submitting a form. You'll create a reset button that will clear the form fields so the user can start over.

1 Click Edit in the Prepare Form toolbar to return to Form Editing mode.

2 Select the Button tool in the Prepare Form toolbar.

3 Click in the upper left corner of the form to create the button.

4 Type **Reset** in the Field Name box, and then click All Properties.

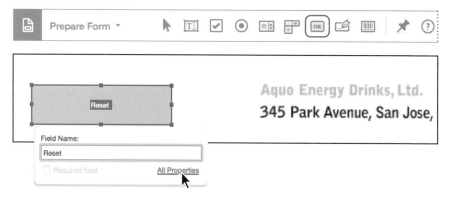

5 Click the Options tab.

6 Type **Start over** in the Label box.

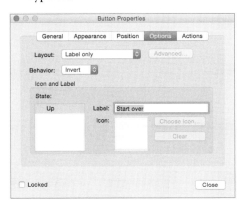

The field name is used to collect and analyze data, but does not appear on the form itself. The label, however, appears in the field when the user is completing the form.

7 Click the Actions tab.

8 Choose Mouse Up from the Select Trigger menu, and then choose Reset A Form from the Select Action menu. Click Add.

When the user clicks the button and releases the mouse (Mouse Up), the form will reset.

9 Click OK in the Reset A Form dialog box to reset the selected fields. By default, all form fields are selected.

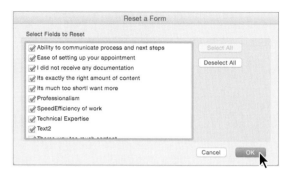

10 Click the Appearance tab.

11 Click the Border Color swatch, and select a shade of blue. In Mac OS, deselect Transparency. Then close the Colors panel.

12 Click the Fill Color swatch, select a shade of gray, and then close the panel.

13 Choose Beveled from the Line Style menu.

The button will appear with a gray background and blue outline, and the beveled line will make it appear to be three-dimensional.

14 Click Close to close the Button Properties dialog box.

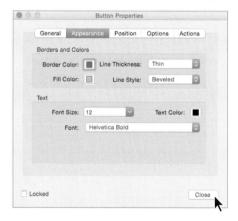

15 Click Preview. Select options for a few questions, and then click the Start Over button you created. The fields reset.

Start over

Aquo Energy Drinks, Ltd.
345 Park Avenue, San Jose,

16 Click Edit to return to form-editing mode.

17 Choose File > Save. If the Save As PDF dialog box appears, save the file with the same name.

Types of form fields

You can include the following types of fields in a PDF form you create in Acrobat:

- **Barcodes** encode the input from selected fields and display it as a visual pattern that can be interpreted by decoding software or hardware (available separately).

- **Buttons** initiate an action on the user's computer, such as opening a file, playing a sound, or submitting data to a web server. You can customize buttons with images, text, and visual changes triggered by moving or clicking a mouse.

- **Check boxes** present yes-or-no choices for individual items. If the form contains multiple check boxes, users can typically select as many of these as they want.

- **Dropdown lists** let the user either choose an item from a pop-up menu or type in a value.

- **Digital signatures** let the user electronically sign a PDF document with a digital signature.

- **List boxes** display a list of options the user can select. You can set a form field property that enables the user to Shift-click, Ctrl-click, or Command-click to select multiple items on the list.

- **Radio buttons** present a group of choices from which the user can select only one item. All radio buttons with the same name work together as a group.

- **Text fields** let the user type in text, such as name, address, email address, or phone number.

Distributing forms

After you have designed and created your form, you can distribute it in several different ways. If you have an email account, you'll send the feedback form to yourself, and then collect the response in email. You'll use the tools in Acrobat to distribute the form.

1   Click Distribute in the right-hand pane.

2   Click Save if you are prompted to save.

3   In the Distribute Form dialog box, select Email, and then click Continue. Click Yes if you are prompted to clear the form before distributing it.

4   In the Distribute Form dialog box, enter or verify your email address, name, title, and organization name, and then click Next. If you've entered that information previously, Acrobat uses the information it has stored.

5   Click Send Using Adobe Acrobat DC, and click Next.

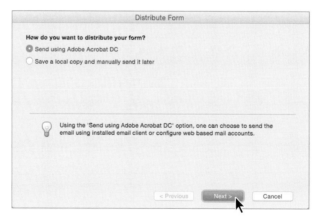

6 Type your email address in the To box. Make sure Collect Name & Email From Recipients To Provide Optimal Tracking is selected. Then click Send.

● **Note:** You can customize the subject line and email message that accompanies your form, and you can send the form to multiple people at once. For the purposes of this lesson, however, you are sending the form only to yourself, with the default message and subject line.

7 In the Send Email dialog box, select Default Email Application if you want to send the message from an email application installed on your computer. If you want to use an online service such as Gmail or Yahoo Mail, select Use Webmail, enter your email address when prompted, and then click OK.

8 Click Continue.

9 If you are sending email through a webmail account, sign in when prompted, read any security messages, and grant access as required. Enter email addresses for recipients, and send the message.

If you choose to send the message through your default email application, Acrobat opens it and sends the message with the attached form.

● **Note:** If you receive a message that you don't have a default email application, click OK. Acrobat then opens the Send Email dialog box.

10 Check your email, and open the attached PDF file to complete the form.

The form opens in Acrobat, and a document message bar appears above it.

The document message bar displays information about the form. If the form does not contain a Submit Form button, one is included in the document message bar. Additionally, the document message bar specifies whether a form is certified or contains signature fields.

● **Note:** If form recipients are using earlier versions of Acrobat or Reader, the document message bar may not be visible or may contain different information.

Tracking forms

If you've used Acrobat to distribute your forms, you can manage the forms that you have distributed or received. Use Tracker to view and edit the location of the response file, track who has responded, add more recipients, email all recipients, and view the responses for a form.

To track forms in Tracker:

1 Open the form you want to track, open the Prepare Form tool, and click Track in the right-hand pane.

Tracker displays reviews you've initiated and forms you've distributed.

2 In the left navigation panel, expand Forms, and click Distributed.

3 Select the form you want to track.

In the main pane, Tracker displays the location of the response file, the method used to distribute the form, the date it was distributed, the list of recipients, and whether each recipient has responded.

4 Do one or more of the following:

- To view all responses for a form, click View Responses.

- To modify the location of the response file, in Response File Location, click Edit File Location.

- To view the original form, click Open Original Form.

- To send the form to more recipients, click Add Recipients.

- To send email to everyone who received the form, click Email All Recipients.

- To remind recipients to complete the form, click Email Recipients Who Haven't Responded.

Options for distributing forms

There are several ways to get your forms to the people who need to fill them out. You can simply post a form on a website, for example, or send it directly from your email application. To take advantage of Acrobat form-management tools to track, collect, and analyze data, use one of these options:

- Send the form as an email attachment, and manually collect responses in your email inbox.

- Send the form using a network folder or a Windows server running Microsoft SharePoint services. You can automatically collect responses on the internal server.

To distribute a form using any of these methods, click Distribute in the Forms panel, and then follow the online instructions. To learn more about distributing forms, see Adobe Acrobat DC Help.

Collecting form data

Electronic forms aren't simply more convenient for users; they also make it easier for you to track, collect, and review form data. When you distribute a form, Acrobat automatically creates a PDF Portfolio for collecting the form data. By default, this file is saved in the same folder as the original form, and is named [filename]_responses.

You'll complete the form and submit it, and then collect the form data.

1 Complete the form you opened, and select options for each question, as if you were the recipient. Type a few words in the multiline field for number 6. Then click Submit Form.

Note: Depending on the security settings in your email application, you may need to approve the message before it is sent.

2 In the Send Form dialog box, verify the email address and name you're using to send the data, and then click Send. Click Continue or Allow if a warning dialog box appears.

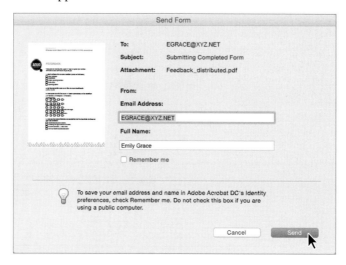

If you receive a message about sending the email, click OK. Depending on settings in your email application, you may need to send the message manually.

3 Check your email. The completed form arrives in a message with the subject line "Submitting Completed Form," or the subject line you used if you mailed it manually. Open the attachment in that message.

4 Select Add to An Existing Response File, and accept the default filename. Then click OK.

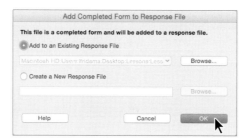

Acrobat compiles the data in the response file that was created when you distributed the form.

5 Click Get Started at the bottom of the PDF Portfolio welcome screen.

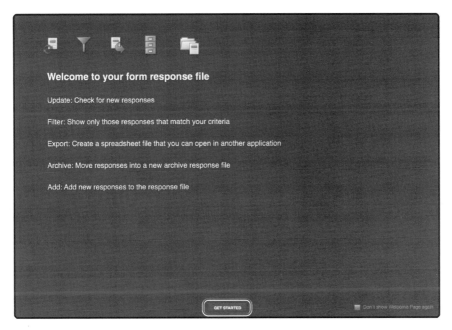

Form data you've collected is listed in the PDF Portfolio. Each response is listed as a separate component. You can use the PDF Portfolio to filter, export, and archive data.

Working with form data

Once your data has been compiled, you can view each response, filter responses according to specific questions, export the data to a CSV or XML file for use in a spreadsheet or database, or archive the data for access later. You'll filter the data from the feedback form and then export it to a CSV file.

● **Note:** You can add multiple form responses to the responses file at once. Click Add, and then navigate to the responses you want to include. With some email applications, you may need to use this method to add files, rather than double-clicking an attachment.

1　Click Filter on the left side of the PDF Portfolio.

2　Scroll down the Select Field Name menu, and choose Other Feedback.

3　Select Is Not Blank from the next menu.

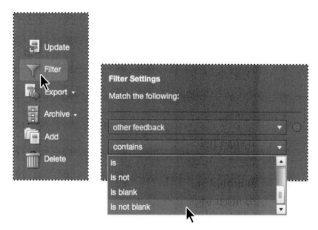

The form you completed is listed, because it contains data in the Other Feedback field.

4　Select Is Blank from the second menu.

The form you completed disappears, because it no longer matches the filter criteria. You can add filters to sort responses based on as many criteria as you like.

5　Select Is Not Blank again, so that your form reappears.

6　Click Done at the bottom of the Filter Settings pane.

7　Select the response.

8　Choose Export > Export Selected on the left side of the PDF Portfolio.

9　Select CSV as the file type, and click Save.

Acrobat creates a comma-separated data file that contains the data from the selected responses. You can open a CSV file in Microsoft Excel or another spreadsheet or database application.

10　Close any open PDF files and Tracker.

Exploring on your own: Calculating and validating numeric fields

Acrobat offers many ways to ensure that users fill out your forms correctly. You can experiment with creating fields that will allow the user to enter only information of a specific type. You can also create fields that automatically calculate values based on entries in other fields.

Validating numeric fields

To ensure that correct information is entered into form fields, use the Acrobat field validation feature. For example, if a response must be a number with a value between 10 and 20, restrict entries to numbers within this range. Here, you'll limit the price of instruments on an order form to no more than $1,000.

1 Choose File > Open, navigate to the Lesson10 folder, and open the Order_Start.pdf file. This PDF file already has form fields in place.

2 Click Prepare Form in the Tools pane to edit the form.

3 Double-click the Price.0 field (the first cell in the Price Each column).

4 In the Text Field Properties dialog box, click the Format tab, and set the following values:

   • For Select Format Category, choose Number.

   • For Decimal Places, choose 2 (to allow cents to be entered).

   • For Separator Style, choose 1,234.56 (the default).

   • For Currency Symbol, choose $ (the dollar sign).

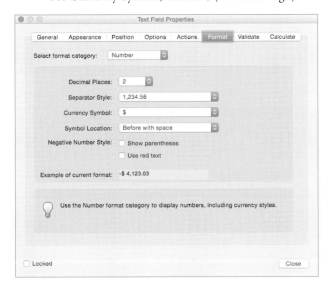

Now you'll specify a validation check on the data entered in this field.

5 Click the Validate tab, and then select Field Value Is In Range. In the range fields, type **0** in the From box and **1000** in the To box. Click Close.

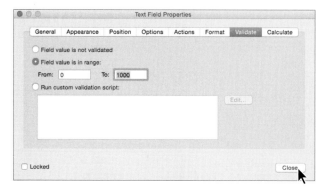

6 Click Preview in the Prepare Form toolbar. Then type **2000** in the field you just edited (the first line in the Price Each column), and press Enter or Return. A message warns you that the entry you have tried to make is unacceptable.

7 Click OK to close the warning dialog box.

Calculating numeric fields

In addition to verifying and formatting form data, you can use Acrobat to calculate values used in form fields. For your PDF order form, you will calculate the cost for each line item, based on the quantity that has been ordered. You will then have Acrobat calculate the total cost of all items that have been ordered.

1 If you're in Preview mode, click Edit.

2 Double-click the Total.0 field (the first cell in the Item Total column).

3 In the Text Field Properties dialog box, click the Calculate tab, and do the following:

  • Select the Value Is The option.

  • For the value, choose Product (x). You'll be multiplying two fields.

  • Click Pick to select the fields to multiply. In the Field Selection dialog box, select the boxes next to Price.0 and Quantity.0. (To scroll through the list of fields, select one, and then press the Down Arrow key.)

4 Click OK to close the Field Selection dialog box, and click Close to exit the Text Field Properties dialog box.

5 Click Preview. Then enter **1.50** for the price and **2** for the quantity in the first row, and press Enter or Return. The Item Total column displays $3.00.

6 Close any open files, and quit Acrobat when you are finished.

Review questions

1 How can you convert an existing document into an interactive PDF form
   in Acrobat DC?

2 What is the difference between a radio button and a button in an interactive
   PDF form?

3 How can you distribute a form to multiple recipients and track the responses
   you receive?

4 Where does Acrobat compile form responses?

Review answers

1 To convert an existing document into an interactive PDF form, open the document
   in Acrobat. Then open the Prepare Form tool, select the current document, and
   click Start.

2 Radio buttons permit the user to select just one of a set of two or more options.
   Buttons trigger actions, such as playing a movie file, going to another page, or clearing
   form data.

3 You can email the form to recipients or post the form on an internal server. Click
   Distribute in the right-hand pane when the Prepare Form tool is open to select a
   distribution option.

4 When you use Acrobat to distribute a form, Acrobat automatically creates a PDF
   Portfolio file for your responses. By default, the file is in the same folder as the original
   form, and the word "_responses" is appended to the name of the original form.

11 USING ACTIONS (ACROBAT PRO)

Lesson overview

This lesson requires Acrobat Pro. In this lesson, you'll do the following:

- Run an action.

- Create an action.

- Create an instruction step for an action.

- Set options in steps so the user doesn't need to provide input.

- Prompt the user for input on specific steps.

- Share an action.

 This lesson will take approximately 45 minutes to complete. Copy the Lesson11 folder onto your hard drive if you haven't already done so.

THOMAS BOOKER
Founder, President and CEO of Aquo

Biography

Thomas Booker founded Aquo Energy Drinks Ltd. in August 2006, and currently acts as the company's President and Chief Executive Officer. Mr. Booker is responsible for overseeing all Aquo business units, including Aquo energy drink and water brands, and also remains a driving force behind Aquo's product development. He has served on the boards of many large public companies, consulting them on environmentally sustainable business practices throughout his career. He currently serves as chairman of the California Corporate Green Building Council. Prior to founding Aquo, Mr. Booker was Director of Research and Development at Purely Natural Energy Company, the ground breaking Northwestern energy bar company that was the first to introduce a 100% organic bar to the national market in 1996. He earned a B.S. from the University of Virginia in 1987, and a MBA from the College of William & Mary in 1990. He was named *Better* magazine's 2006 "Most Environmentally Responsible CEO of the Year."

Actions in Adobe Acrobat DC Pro automate tasks and make processes more consistent. You can use the actions that come with Acrobat or create your own to use and share.

About actions

In Adobe Acrobat DC Pro, you can use actions to automate multistep tasks and share processes with others. An action is a collection of steps: Some steps, such as adding tags to a document, can be performed automatically by Acrobat. Some steps, such as removing hidden information, require input as to which information to remove or add, or which settings to use. Other steps, such as adding bookmarks, cannot be done automatically because you need to use human discretion to create and name the bookmarks; in those cases, an action includes instructions for the user to perform the necessary step before the action continues.

Acrobat Pro includes several actions in the Action Wizard tool. You can use these actions to perform common tasks, such as preparing documents for distribution or creating accessible PDFs. You can also create your own actions, assembling steps in the order that works for your process, and including informational steps where appropriate for the people who will be using each action.

Actions that contain automated steps are particularly useful for tasks you perform frequently. Actions in general are handy for tasks you perform less frequently, but which require the same steps each time. Using actions, you can ensure that critical steps are included in the process.

Using predefined actions

To use an action, open the Action Wizard tool, and select the action in the Actions list in the right-hand pane. To gain practice using actions, you'll use the Prepare For Distribution action to prepare a document before posting it on an external website.

1   Start Acrobat Pro, and choose File > Open. Navigate to the Lesson11 folder, select Aquo_CEO.pdf, and click Open.

The Aquo_CEO.pdf document is a biography of the chief executive of a fictitious beverage company.

2   Click Tools, and then click Action Wizard to open it.

3 Select Prepare For Distribution in the Actions List in the right-hand pane.

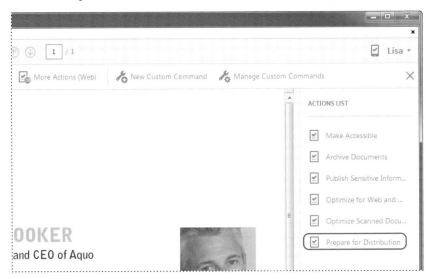

The action steps and information appear where the Actions List was. The action pane names the files to be processed, lets you add files if you want to, and then lists the steps and information for the action itself.

4 Review the steps for this action. When you've read the information, click Start to proceed to the first step.

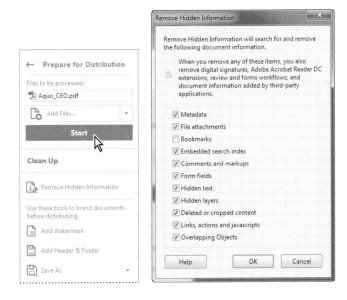

The Start button changes to a Stop button, which you can click at any time to stop the action. The Remove Hidden Information dialog box appears, and that step is highlighted in the action pane.

5   Click OK in the Remove Hidden Information dialog box to accept the default selections.

6   In the Add Watermark dialog box, click an insertion point in the Text box. Then type **Copyright Aquo 2015**. Select 20 for the font size, and set the Opacity to 25%. In the Position area of the dialog box, enter **1** point for the Vertical Distance, and choose Bottom from the From menu. Then choose Right from the From menu for Horizontal Distance. The watermark should appear in the lower right corner of the document in the Preview pane. Click OK to accept the watermark.

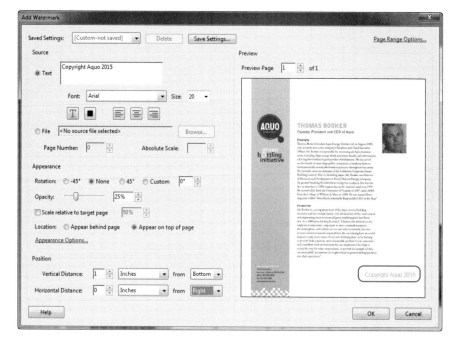

7 In the Add Header And Footer dialog box, click an insertion point in the Center Header Text box, and then type **Aquo Corporate Information**. Change the font size to 9. The header appears in the preview area. Click OK to add the header and close the dialog box.

▶ **Tip:** To add a header or footer when you're not using an action, open the Edit PDF tool, and choose Header & Footer > Add.

8 In the Save As dialog box, name the document **Aquo_CEO_dist.pdf**, and click Save.

The action pane now shows the word Completed where the Stop button was.

9 Click Full Report at the bottom of the action pane to see an itemized list of the tasks performed by the action. The report opens in a browser window. When you're done reviewing it, close the browser.

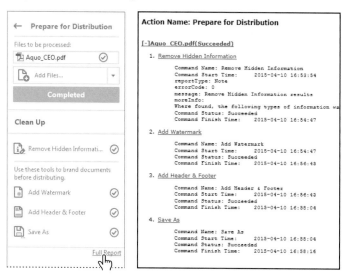

10 In Acrobat Pro, leave the Action Wizard tool and the document open.

Creating an action

You can create your own actions, assembling Acrobat steps and instructional steps to automate a process or to make it more consistent. Before you create an action, consider the steps involved and the logical order for those steps. For example, encrypting a document with password protection should be among the last steps in the action.

You'll create an action for preparing a multimedia presentation in Acrobat DC Pro. The steps you'll include are adding a header or footer to visually link the pages to each other, adding video files, creating page transitions, setting the file to open in Full Screen mode, and then adding a password to the document to prevent others from making changes.

1 In the Action Wizard toolbar, click New Action.

The Create New Action dialog box is divided into two panes. The left pane displays tools that you can include in the action (arranged by category). In the right pane of the dialog box are options for files to be processed and the steps you've added to the action. Use the buttons on the far right to design the action's appearance; you can add dividers, panels, and instructions.

2 In the Create New Action dialog box, make sure Add Files is chosen from the Default Option menu.

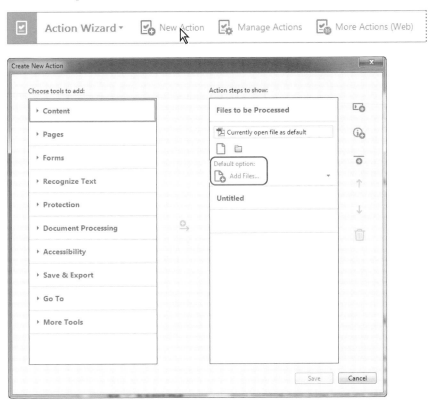

You can apply an action to an open file, or the action can prompt the user to select a file or folder, require the user to scan a document, or open a file from cloud storage.

Adding steps to an action

▶ **Tip:** If you change your mind about a step, you can delete it. Select the step, and then click the Remove button (🗑) on the right side of the dialog box. To change the order of steps, use the Move Up and Move Down buttons.

Now you're ready to add the steps.

1   Expand the Pages category in the left pane of the dialog box, and select Add Header & Footer.

2   Click the Add To Right-Hand Pane button (⊙→) in the middle of the dialog box. The Add Header & Footer step appears in the panel in the list on the right.

3   Select Prompt User for the step. When the action runs, the user can customize the header or footer for the presentation.

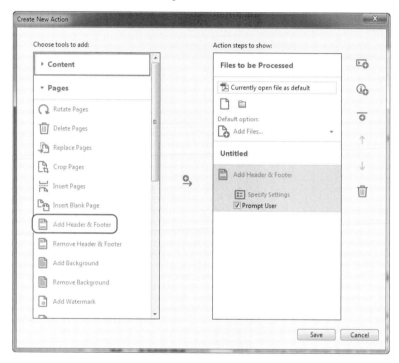

The next step is to add video files. There is no Add Video step available in the Create New Action dialog box, so you'll add an instruction step for the user.

4   Click the Add Instruction button (ℹ) on the right side of the dialog box.

5 In the Add Or Edit Label dialog box, type **Add video files as appropriate. To add a video, click Add Video in the Rich Media toolbar, drag a box on the page, and select the video file and any settings.** Then click Save.

You can add as much or as little information as you want in an instruction step. If you're sharing your action with people who are less familiar with Acrobat, consider providing detailed steps. If you're creating an action for yourself, a reminder to perform the step, such as "Add video," may be enough.

6 Click Pause for the step you created to give the user time to read your instructions.

While an action is running, you can't access the Tools pane or the Tools Center. So if you need users to access a tool, add a Go To step. In this case, you want the user to use the Rich Media tool to add a video.

7 Expand the Go To category, and double-click Rich Media.

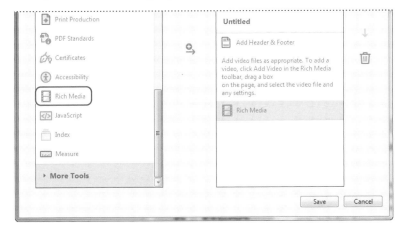

8 Expand the Document Processing category in the left pane, and double-click Page Transitions.

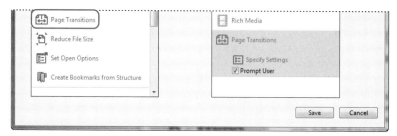

When you double-click an option on the left side, it's automatically added as a step on the right.

9 Click the Specify Settings button in the Page Transitions step.

10 Choose Dissolve from the Transition menu, and then choose Medium from the Speed menu. Then click OK.

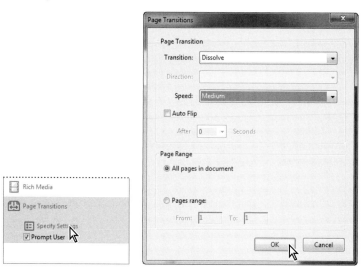

11 Deselect Prompt User in the Page Transitions step.

Acrobat will automatically apply the options you select for the Page Transitions step, without prompting the user.

12 In the left pane, double-click Set Open Options in the Document Processing category.

13 Deselect Prompt User, and then click the Specify Settings button for the new step. In the Set Open Options dialog box, choose Yes from the Open In Full Screen Mode menu, and then click OK.

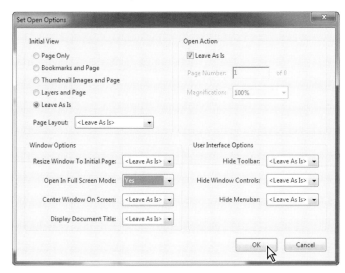

14 Expand the Protection category, and then double-click Encrypt. Select Prompt User in the Encrypt step so that each user can set an individual password.

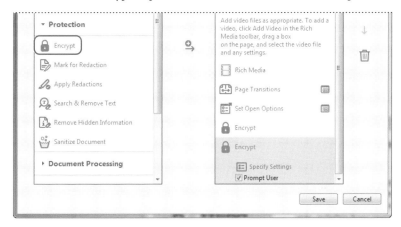

Saving an action

When you've added all the steps, confirmed that they're in the appropriate order, and specified the options you want, save and name the action.

1 Click Save.

2 Name the action **Prepare Multimedia Presentation**.

3 For the action description, type **Add video, headers, transitions, and a password to a presentation**. Then click Save.

Give actions names that help you remember what the actions do. It's usually a good idea, especially if you'll be sharing the action, to describe the product of the action or when you should use it, such as when you're preparing documents for a particular client or purpose.

Testing an action

Now you'll test-drive your action to ensure it works the way you expect. You'll create a multimedia presentation for a fictitious beverage company.

1 Choose File > Open, and open the Aquo_presentation.pdf file in the Lesson11 folder.

2 Click Tools, and then open the Action Wizard tool.

3 In the Actions List, select Prepare Multimedia Presentation. The action steps replace the Actions List, and the open document is the default file to be processed.

4   Click Start to proceed to the first step in the action.

5   In the Add Header And Footer dialog box, click an insertion point in the Left Header Text box, and then type **Aquo Shareholders Meeting 2015**. Change the font size to 10, and then click OK.

The instruction step you created appears on the screen. Because you selected the Pause option for the step, the user must click Click To Proceed in order to continue working through the action. You'll add a video.

6   Click Click To Proceed in the instruction box. Acrobat opens the Rich Media tool and presents another informational message at the bottom of the application window.

7 Click Add Video in the Rich Media toolbar. Drag a box over the right half of the bottle ad page (the first page in the document). Click Browse or Choose, select the Aquo_T03_Loop.mp4 file from the Lesson11 folder, and click Open. Then click OK.

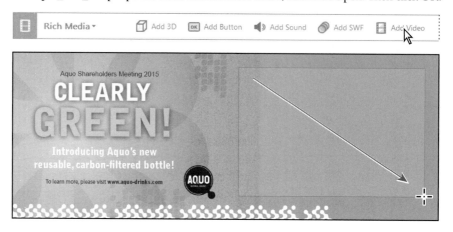

8 Click the Play button to preview the video file. When you're done, click the Pause button to stop it. Then click Click To Proceed in the informational box to proceed to the next step.

Acrobat automatically performs the next two steps—adding page transitions and setting the presentation to open in Full Screen mode—because no input is required. The final step is adding a password, which does require input.

9 In the Document Security dialog box, choose Password Security from the Security Method menu. In the Permissions area of the Password Security – Settings dialog box, select Restrict Editing And Printing Of the Document. In the Change Permissions Password box, enter **Aquo1234** as the password. Then click OK.

Avoiding the Full Screen mode warning

By default, Acrobat warns you when a PDF file is set to be opened in Full Screen mode, because it is possible for malicious programmers to create PDF files that appear to be other applications. If you click Remember My Choice For This Document, Acrobat will not show the warning again when you open the presentation on this computer. If you are presenting material on your own computer, you can change the preference so that Acrobat will not display the warning at the beginning of your presentation. To change the preference, choose Edit > Preferences (Windows) or Acrobat > Preferences (Mac OS), and then click Full Screen on the left. Deselect the Alert When Document Requests Full Screen option.

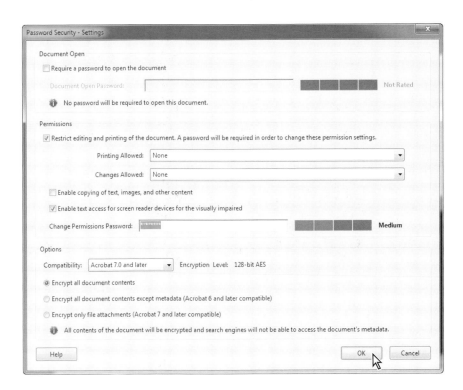

10 Click OK in the informational dialog box, enter the password again when prompted, and then click OK. Click Close to close the Document Security dialog box.

Acrobat reports that the Prepare Multimedia Presentation action has been completed.

11 Choose File > Save As, name the presentation file **Aquo_meeting.pdf**, and then click Save.

12 Close the document file, but leave Aquo_CEO_dist.pdf open. If you want to see the presentation open in Full Screen mode with its header and page transitions, open the Aquo_meeting.pdf file in Acrobat. When you're done, press the Esc key to exit Full Screen mode, and then close the file.

Sharing actions

▶ **Tip:** You can edit actions after you create them: Click Manage Actions. In the Manage Actions dialog box, select the action name, and click Edit.

You can share actions you create or edit with other users.

1 If the Action Wizard tool isn't open, open it.

2 Click Manage Actions in the Action Wizard toolbar.

3 Select the Prepare Multimedia Presentation action, and click Export.

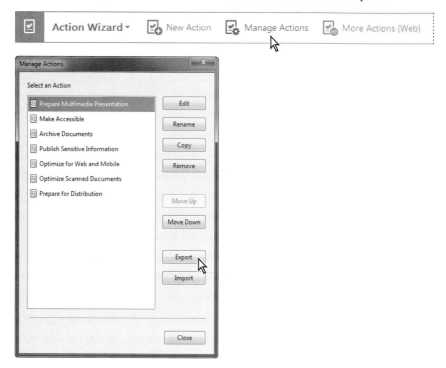

4 Name the action **Prepare Multimedia Presentation** (the default name), save it in the Lesson11 folder, and click Save.

The action file is saved with an .sequ extension. You can copy .sequ files or email them to other users. To open an .sequ file that someone has sent you, click Import in the Manage Actions dialog box, and select the action file.

5 Click Close to close the Manage Actions dialog box. Then close any open documents, and quit Acrobat.

Review questions

1 What is an action in Acrobat DC Pro?

2 How can you create a step in an action if the step isn't available in the left pane of the Create New Action dialog box?

3 How can you share an action with others?

Review answers

1 An action is a collection of steps: Some steps, such as adding tags to a document, can be performed automatically by Acrobat. Some steps, such as removing hidden information, require input as to what to remove or add, or which settings to use. Other steps, such as adding bookmarks, cannot be done automatically, because you need to use human discretion to create and name the bookmarks.

2 To include a step that isn't predefined in Acrobat, click the Add Instruction button, and then type instructions to the user.

3 To share an action, click Manage Actions in the Action Wizard toolbar, select the action you want to share, and click Export. Then send the resulting .sequ file to the person you want to share the action with.

12 USING ACROBAT IN PROFESSIONAL PRINTING

Lesson overview

In this lesson, you'll do the following:

- Create Adobe PDF files suitable for high-resolution printing.

- Preflight an Adobe PDF file to check for quality and consistency (Acrobat Pro).

- View how transparent objects affect a page (Acrobat Pro).

- Configure color management.

- Use Acrobat to generate color separations.

 This lesson will take approximately 60 minutes to complete. Copy the Lesson12 folder onto your hard drive if you haven't already done so.

METHOD & PROCESS

Self reinvention is something we all entertain, and the way fashion allows us to dream.

Alice Ritter is kneeling at the feet of a long-limbed model, one of a dozen milling around a photography set in clothes from her Fall-Winter 2011 collection. It is crucial that she get the girl's pant legs scrunched just so for the shoot. Precise, but with an unstudied symmetry that somehow comes off as casual. She readily admits to being obsessed with this level of detail, because it's where story springs from. "Design is storytelling," Ritter explains. "You start to draw, then you go into the details and the story takes over."

As much as detail is the motor that drives the story inherent in an Alice Ritter piece, it's also what provokes an emotional response to the item. "The piece has to trigger an emotion," Ritter believes, and the seat of emotion is detail. Detail grabs you by the scruff of the neck. It slips its hand in yours. It follows you home. Detail is what makes an item "really special," she says, "the one dress you'll wear for ten years."

So she sweats the small stuff, crafting and editing a fresh batch of stories with each new collection. The unifying design element--the signature plotline threading one season to the next--is the vision of a better Alice. One who regularly tumbles down the rabbit hole to see where the

path might lead her. The story she's telling and the design process that leads her there is "a reflection of my journey, my self-discovery. A big part of my identity—or my dreamed identity—goes into my design."

Which raises a really good question: Who is Alice Ritter anyway? There are at least two ways to tell that story.

A small-town French girl raised in a nice family with traditional bourgeois values, she grew up playing dress up in her grandparents' attic with a cache of 19th century gowns and corsets. While that piqued her interest in fashion early on, the couture in the pages of French Vogue—Chanel, Yves Saint Laurent and Balmain and the rest—hooked her for life on design. "I

Acrobat Pro provides professional printing tools, including preflighting and transparency previews, to help you achieve high-quality output.

Creating PDF files for print and prepress

As you learned in Lesson 2, there are many ways to create a PDF file from your original document. No matter which method you choose, however, you need to use the appropriate PDF preset for your intended output. For high-resolution, professional printing, specify the Press Quality PDF preset or a custom PDF preset provided by your printer.

About Adobe PDF presets

A PDF preset is a group of settings that affect the process of creating a PDF file. These settings are designed to balance file size with quality, depending on how the PDF file will be used. Most predefined presets are shared across Adobe Creative Cloud applications, including Adobe InDesign, Adobe Illustrator, Adobe Photoshop, and Acrobat. You can also create and share custom presets to meet your own needs.

Presets that include "(Japan)" in their names are specifically designed for Japanese print workflows. For more detailed descriptions of each preset, see Adobe Acrobat DC Help.

- **High Quality Print** creates PDFs for quality printing on desktop printers and proofing devices.

- **Oversized Pages** creates PDFs suitable for viewing and printing engineering drawings larger than 200 by 200 inches.

- **PDF/A-1b (CMYK and RGB)** standards are used for the long-term preservation (archival) of electronic documents.

- **PDF/X-1a** standards minimize the number of variables in a PDF document to improve reliability. PDF/X-1a files are commonly used for digital ads that will be reproduced on a press.

- **PDF/X-3** files are similar to PDF/X-1a files, but they support color-managed workflows and allow some RGB images.

- **PDF/X-4** has the same color-management ICC color specifications as PDF/X-3, but includes support for live transparency.

- **Press Quality** creates PDF files for high-quality print production (for example, for digital printing or for separations to an imagesetter or platesetter).

- **Smallest File Size** creates PDF files for displaying on the web or an intranet, or for distribution through an email system.

- **Standard** creates PDF files to be printed to desktop printers or digital copiers, published on a CD, or sent to a client as a publishing proof.

Guidelines for creating print-ready PDF files

By the time you submit a PDF file to a printer, the die has been cast. A printer can coax a quality print-out from some less-than-optimal PDF files, but for the most part, the printer is restricted by decisions made during the creative process. Following these guidelines, you can deliver the strongest, highest-quality PDF file to a printer:

- **Remember that the end product is only as good as its components.** For high-quality printing, a PDF file must contain the appropriate images, fonts, and other components.

- **Convert only when absolutely necessary.** Every time you convert text, objects, or color, you compromise the integrity of the file. The printed product will most closely resemble your original intent if you minimize conversions. Keep text in its original form, as fonts, rather than outlining or rasterizing it. Keep gradients live. Maintain live transparency as long as possible. And don't convert colors from device-independent or high-gamut color spaces, such as RGB, to device-specific or low-gamut color spaces, such as CMYK, unless advised to do so.

- **Use transparency efficiently.** Transparency comes into play any time you apply a blending mode or change the opacity of an object. For the best results, keep transparency live as long as possible; place objects you don't want the flattener to affect (such as text and line objects) above all nearby sources of transparency, preferably on a separate layer; and use the highest quality flattener settings if and when you flatten transparency.

- **Proof and preflight before creating the PDF file.** Early in the workflow, you have more context for problems, and more options for fixing them. Carefully proof the content and formatting before creating a PDF file. Additionally, if the authoring application provides a preflight feature, use it to identify missing fonts, unlinked images, or other issues that could result in problems down the road. The earlier you can identify and fix a problem, the easier and less expensive it is to fix. Certainly, technical problems found while you're still working in the authoring program are easier to fix than problems found in Acrobat or on a printing press.

- **Embed fonts.** To minimize the chance of complications, embed fonts in the PDF file. Read the end user license agreement (EULA) before purchasing a font to ensure it permits embedding.

- **Use the appropriate PDF settings file.** When you create the PDF file, make sure you're using the appropriate settings. The PDF settings file determines how image data is saved, whether fonts are embedded, and whether colors are converted. By default, Acrobat PDFMaker in Microsoft Office creates PDF files using the Standard settings file, which does not meet the requirements for most high-end printing. No matter what application you're using to create a PDF file for professional printing, ensure that you're using the PDF/X-1a or Press Quality PDF settings file, or the settings file recommended by your printer.

- **Create a PDF/X file if appropriate.** PDF/X is a subset of the Adobe PDF specification, requiring that PDF files meet specific criteria for the printing industry, resulting in more reliable PDF files. Using PDF/X-compliant files eliminates the most common errors in file preparation: fonts that aren't embedded, incorrect color spaces, and overprinting issues. PDF/X-1a, PDF/X-3, and PDF/X-4 are the most popular formats; each is designed for a different purpose. Ask your printer whether you should save your file in a PDF/X format.

Creating the PDF file

You can create a PDF file from any application using the Print command. Because we do not know which applications you use, we have not included a file for this exercise. You can use any existing document or create a new document.

1   Open any document in its original application.

Note: Some applications don't use the standard Print dialog boxes to create PDF files. For example, to save a PDF file from Adobe InDesign, use the Export command.

2   Choose File > Print.

3   Do one of the following:

In Windows: Choose Adobe PDF from the list of available printers. Then click Properties, Preferences, or Setup, depending on the application. Choose Press Quality or a custom PDF settings file.

In Mac OS: Click PDF, and choose Save As Adobe PDF from the menu. Then, in the Save As Adobe PDF dialog box, select the Press Quality settings file or a custom settings file from the Adobe PDF Settings menu, and click Continue.

4   In Windows, choose Prompt For Adobe PDF Filename from the Adobe PDF Output Folder menu, and then click OK. If you do not select this option, the Adobe PDF printer saves the file in the My Documents folder. (In Mac OS, you will be prompted for a filename and location automatically.)

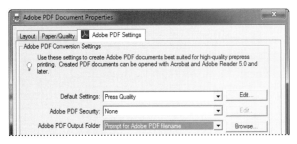

5   In Windows, click Print.

6 Specify a filename and folder for the PDF file when prompted, and click Save.

7 Close the PDF file and the original document.

For more information about selecting presets, see Adobe Acrobat DC Help.

Preflighting files (Acrobat Pro)

Before you hand off a PDF file to a print service provider, preflight it to verify that the document meets the criteria for print publishing. Preflighting analyzes a document against the criteria listed in the preflight profile you specify; in addition to identifying potential issues, many preflight profiles contain fixups that can correct problems for you.

Ask your print service provider which preflight profile to use to accurately preflight your document. Many print service providers provide custom preflight profiles to their customers.

You'll preflight a file to determine whether it's ready for digital printing.

1 In Acrobat Pro, choose File > Open, and navigate to the Lesson12 folder. Select the Profile.pdf file, and click Open.

2 Click Tools to open the Tools Center. Then, choose Add Shortcut in the menu beneath the Print Production tool to add the tool to the Tools pane. You'll use the tool multiple times in this lesson.

3 In the Tools pane, click Print Production.

4 Click Preflight in the right-hand pane.

The Preflight dialog box lists the available preflight profiles, grouped into categories that describe the tests they perform.

5   Click the triangle next to Digital Printing And Online Publishing to expand the category.

6   Select the Digital Printing (Color) profile.

The full magnifying glass icon next to the profile indicates that it performs analysis; the full wrench icon indicates that it also performs fixups. When you select the profile, Acrobat displays its description. If a profile does not include analysis, or checks, the magnifying glass appears as an outline. If a profile does not include fixups, the wrench appears as an outline.

7   Click Analyze And Fix.

8   In the Save As PDF File dialog box, name the fixed file **Profile_fixed.pdf,** and click Save.

Because the profile applies fixups, it makes changes to the file. Saving the file to a different name ensures that you can return to the original if you need to.

9   Review the results of the preflight.

Acrobat displays the results of the preflight in the Results pane. In this file, Acrobat performed several fixups, applying compression, color conversion, and transparency flattening, as well as other changes.

The Results pane also notes that a white object is not set to knock out and that some objects use RGB colors. If you were professionally printing this document, you might want to contact your print service provider to ensure that these factors won't cause problems when your document is printed.

10 Click Create Report.

11 Click Save to save the report in the Lesson12 folder with the default name **Profile_fixed_report.pdf**.

Acrobat creates the preflight summary report as a PDF and opens it in Acrobat.

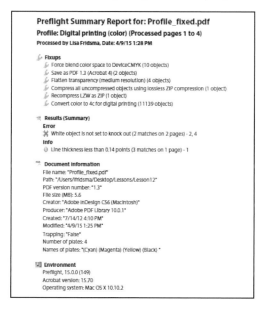

12 Close the Preflight dialog box, and review the preflight summary report.

You can send the preflight summary report to your print service provider if you have any questions about preparing the file. Note that there are five pages to the report: The first page provides a summary of fixups and errors. The summary page is followed by the document itself, with comments identifying where the errors occur.

13 Choose File > Close to close the preflight summary report, and then choose File > Close again to close the Profile_fixed.pdf file.

Tip: You can hide or show individual layers that were created in the authoring application, and determine which ones will print. To learn about showing, hiding, and printing layers, see Adobe Acrobat DC Help.

Working with transparency (Acrobat Pro)

Adobe applications let you modify objects in ways that can affect the underlying artwork, creating the appearance of transparency. You may create transparency by using an opacity slider in InDesign, Illustrator, or Photoshop, or by changing the blending mode for a layer or selected object. Transparency also comes into play whenever you create a drop shadow or apply feathering. Adobe applications can keep transparency "live," or editable, as you move documents from one application to another, but transparency must typically be flattened before printing. In Acrobat Pro, you can see which areas of your document are affected by transparency, and how those areas will print.

Previewing transparency

Note: If your print service provider is using a RIP that includes the Adobe PDF Print Engine, you may not need to flatten transparency.

When you print to most printers, transparency is flattened. The flattening process separates overlapping areas of artwork into discrete sections that are converted either into separate vector shapes or rasterized pixels to retain the look of the transparency.

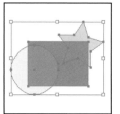

Objects before flattening   Objects after flattening
(Overlapping art is divided when flattened.)

Before flattening occurs, you can determine how much of the transparent area remains vector, and how much becomes rasterized. Some effects, such as drop shadows, must be rasterized in order to print correctly.

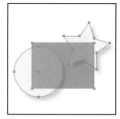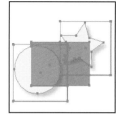

If you received a PDF file created by someone else, you may not know if or where transparency has been applied. The Acrobat transparency preview shows you where transparency is used in a document. This feature can also help you determine the best flattener settings to use when printing the document.

▶ **Tip:** In Acrobat DC Pro, you can quickly see whether a PDF file includes transparency: Select Output Preview in the Print Production panel. At the bottom of the Output Preview dialog box, Acrobat reports whether the page has transparency. If it doesn't, there's no need to flatten it.

PDF standards

PDF standards are internationally defined standards designed to simplify the exchange of graphic content (PDF/X), archived documents (PDF/A), or engineering workflows (PDF/E). The most widely used standards for a print publishing workflow are PDF/X-1a, PDF/X-3, and PDF/X-4.

You can validate PDF content against PDF/X, PDF/A, or PDF/E criteria in Acrobat Pro and save a copy of the document as PDF/X, PDF/A, or PDF/E, provided it complies with the specified requirements. You can also save a PDF file as a PDF/X or PDF/A file when you create the file using the Print command or the Export or Save command in an Adobe application.

In Acrobat DC or Acrobat Reader DC, you can use the Standards pane to see information about the file's conformance. The Standards pane is available only if an open document conforms to a standard; choose View > Show/Hide > Navigation Panes > Standards to open it. If you are using Acrobat DC Pro, you can also click Verify Conformance in the Standards pane to verify that the PDF file is a valid PDF/X or PDF/A file, using the preflight feature.

To save a copy of an existing PDF file as a PDF/X , PDF/A, or PDF/E file in Acrobat DC Pro:

1   Choose File > Save As.

2   Select a destination folder for the file.

3   In the Save As dialog box, choose PDF/A, PDF/E, or PDF/X from the Save As Type or Format menu, and click Settings.

4   Select the version of the standard and any other options, and click OK.

5   In the Save As dialog box, name the converted file, and click Save.

Acrobat converts the file, displaying messages about its progress.

You'll preview transparency in the Profile.pdf file.

1 Open the Profile.pdf file from the Lesson12 folder.

2 Navigate to page 1 of the document. If the entire page is not visible, choose View > Zoom > Zoom To Page Level.

3 Open the Print Production tool, and then click Flattener Preview in the right-hand pane.

The Flattener Preview shows a preview of page 1 of the document on the right side of the dialog box.

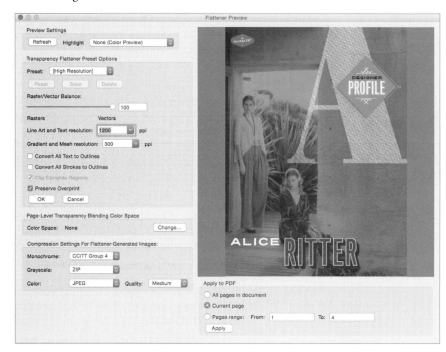

Specifying flattener preview settings

You can select different settings to preview different aspects of the way transparency interacts with objects in the document.

1 In the Flattener Preview dialog box, choose All Affected Objects from the Highlight menu. Nearly the entire page is highlighted in red, indicating that the objects themselves have transparent properties or interact with objects that have transparent properties. Only a few items, including the text at the bottom of the page, are not affected by transparency.

What is rasterization?

Rasterization is the process of changing vector objects, including fonts, into bitmap images to display or print them. The number of pixels per inch (ppi) is referred to as the *resolution*. The higher the resolution in a raster image, the better the quality. When flattening occurs, some objects may need to be rasterized, depending upon flattening settings.

Vector Object

Rasterized at 72 ppi

Rasterized at 300 ppi

2 Choose High Resolution from the Preset menu in the Transparency Flattener Preset Options area. The preset determines how much of the artwork remains vector and how much is rasterized. For professional printing, use the High Resolution preset unless your print service provider advises you differently.

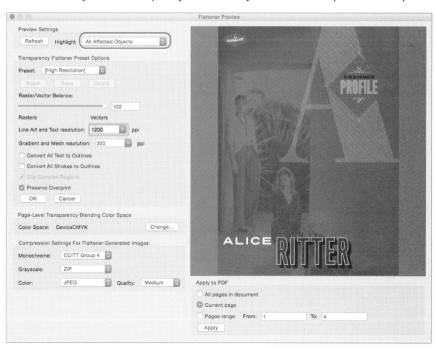

3 Click the left end of the Raster/Vector Balance slider, or type **0** in the box. Then click Refresh in the Preview Settings area, and choose All Affected Objects from the Highlight menu. Everything on the page is highlighted in red, indicating that everything would be rasterized at this setting.

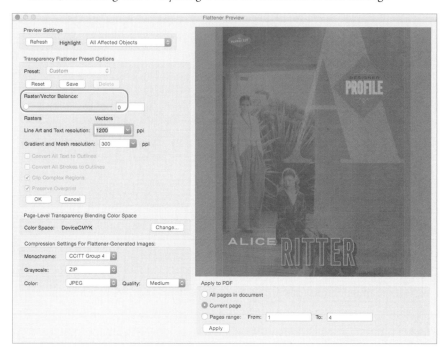

▶ **Tip:** You can find more information about printing transparency on the Adobe website at www.adobe.com.

4 Make other selections to see how the settings affect the document. When you are finished, click the close button in the upper right (Windows) or upper left (Mac OS) corner of the window to close the Flattener Preview window without applying your settings.

If you want to use the selected transparency flattener settings when printing, click Apply in the Flattener Preview dialog box.

About flattening options in the Flattener Preview dialog box

- **Line Art And Text Resolution** determines the resolution at which line art and text are rasterized. Because line art and text involve a sharper contrast around the edges, they need to be rasterized at a higher resolution to maintain a high-quality appearance. A resolution of 300 ppi is sufficient when proofing, but this should be increased to a higher resolution for final high-quality output. A resolution of 1200 ppi is typically sufficient for high-quality output.

- **Gradient And Mesh Resolution** determines the resolution at which radients and meshes, which are sometimes called *blends*, will be rasterized. The resolution should be set appropriately for your specific printer. For proofing to a general-purpose laser printer or inkjet printer, the default setting of 150 ppi is appropriate. For printing to most high-quality output devices, such as a film or plate output device, a resolution of 300 ppi is usually sufficient.

- **Convert All Text To Outlines** ensures that the weight of all text in the artwork stays consistent. However, converting small fonts to outlines can make them appear noticeably thicker and less readable (especially when printing on lower-end printing systems).

- **Convert All Strokes To Outlines** ensures that the weight of all strokes in the artwork stays consistent. Selecting this option, however, causes thin strokes to appear slightly thicker (especially when printing on lower-end printing systems).

- **Clip Complex Regions** ensures that the boundaries between vector artwork and rasterized artwork fall along object paths. This option reduces stitching artifacts that result when part of an object is rasterized while another part remains in vector form (as determined by the Raster/Vector slider). Selecting this option may result in extremely complex clipping paths, which take significant time to compute, and can cause errors when printing.

- **Preserve Overprint** blends the color of transparent artwork with the background color to create an overprint effect. Overprinted colors are two or more inks printed on top of each other. For example, when a cyan ink prints over a yellow ink, the resulting overprint is a green color. Without overprinting, the underlying yellow would not be printed, resulting in a cyan color.

Setting up color management

Using color management can help you achieve consistent color throughout your workflow. Color profiles describe the characteristics of each device. Color management uses those profiles to map the colors possible for one device, such as a computer monitor, with the colors possible on another device, such as a printer.

1   Choose Edit > Preferences (Windows) or Acrobat > Preferences (Mac OS), and select Color Management from the list on the left.

2   From the Settings menu, choose North America Prepress 2. With this setting, Acrobat displays colors as they generally appear when printed using North American printing standards.

● **Note:** You can synchronize color management settings for all the Adobe Creative Cloud applications in Adobe Bridge, which is available as part of a Creative Cloud subscription. See Bridge Help for more information.

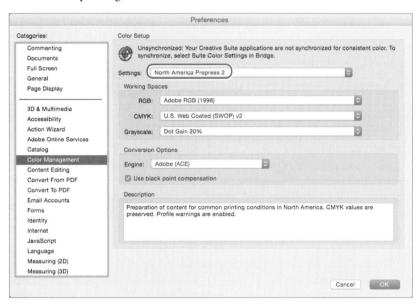

The setting you select determines which color working spaces are used by the application and how the color management system converts colors. To view a description of a setting, select the setting, and then position the pointer over the setting name. The description appears at the bottom of the dialog box.

ACE (Adobe Color Engine) is the same color management engine used by other Adobe graphics software, so you can be confident that color management settings applied in Acrobat will mirror those applied in your other Adobe applications.

3   Click OK to close the Preferences dialog box.

Previewing your print job (Acrobat Pro)

You've already previewed how transparency will print. Now you'll preview color separations and verify the resolution of individual objects. You'll also perform a *soft proof*—that is, you'll proof the document on the screen without having to print it.

Previewing color separations

To reproduce color and continuous-tone images, printers usually separate artwork into four plates, called *process colors*—one plate for each of the cyan, magenta, yellow, and black portions of the image. You can also include custom pre-mixed inks, called *spot colors*, which require their own plates. When inked with the appropriate color and printed in register with one another, these colors combine to reproduce the original artwork. The plates are called *color separations*.

You will preview color separations from this document using the Output Preview dialog box.

1   Make sure you're viewing page 1 of the document, and that the Print Production tool is open.

2   Click Output Preview in the right-hand pane.

3   Choose Separations from the Preview menu.

The Separations area of the dialog box lists all the inks that are included in this document for printing. There are four process inks (cyan, magenta, yellow, and black) and two spot colors (TOYO 0349 and TOYO 0343).

4   Drag the Output Preview dialog box to the side so that you can see the document. Then, in the Output Preview dialog box, deselect every ink except TOYO 0349. The items that remain on the page use the selected ink.

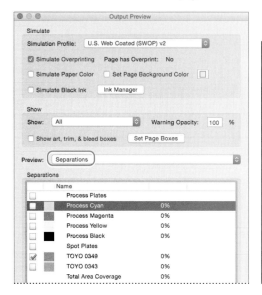

5   Deselect TOYO 0349, and select Process Magenta. Only those items that would print on the magenta plate appear.

▶ **Tip:** If you wanted to remap a spot color to a process color in order to limit the number of plates, and thus the expense, of a print job, you could use the Ink Manager, also available in the Output Preview dialog box.

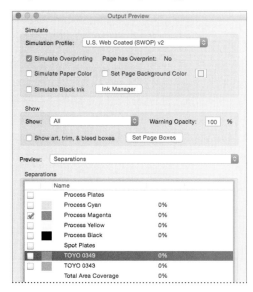

6   Select all the inks again.

Soft-proofing your document

You can use the Output Preview dialog box to soft-proof a document, so that you can see onscreen how your document will look when printed. Use the simulation settings to approximate the color.

As you change the profile chosen in the Simulation Profile menu, color shifts on the monitor. When you soft-proof a document, select the simulation profile that matches your output device. If you use accurately calibrated ICC profiles and have calibrated your monitor, the onscreen preview should match the final output. If you haven't calibrated your monitor or your profiles, the preview may not provide an exact match. For information about calibrating your monitor and profiles, see Adobe Acrobat DC Help.

● **Note:** If you're working with a PDF/X or PDF/A file, the color profile that is embedded in the file as its output intent is automatically selected.

Inspecting objects in a PDF file

You can take a closer look at individual graphics and text in a PDF file using the Object Inspector. The Object Inspector displays the image resolution, color mode, transparency, and other information about the selected object.

You'll check the resolution of the image on page 2.

1 Choose Object Inspector from the Preview menu in the Output Preview dialog box.

2 Scroll to page 2, and click the image of the woman.

Tip: You can document the information the Object Inspector reports for easy access later. Shift-click an area to create a comment with that information.

The Object Inspector lists attributes of the image you clicked, including the image resolution: 274.543 by 274.543 pixels.

3 Click the body text on the page. The Object Inspector displays information about the text, including the font and type size.

4 Close the Output Preview dialog box, and then close the Print Production tool.

Advanced printing controls

Tip: Overprinting is automatically displayed accurately in PDF/X files in all versions of Acrobat DC and Acrobat Reader DC. You can change the settings to display overprinting accurately for all files in the Page Display pane of the Acrobat Preferences dialog box.

You'll use the advanced printing features of Acrobat DC Pro to produce color separations, add printing marks, and control how transparent and complex items are imaged.

1 Choose File > Print.

2 In the Print dialog box, choose a PostScript printer. In Windows, if you do not have a PostScript printer available, you can choose Adobe PDF.

Some advanced printing options, including color separations, are available only for PostScript printers. The Adobe PDF printer uses a PostScript printer driver, so it provides access to the options covered in this exercise.

3 In the Pages To Print area, select All.

4 In the Page Sizing & Handling area, select Fit.

The Fit option reduces or enlarges each page to fit the paper size.

5 Click Advanced.

There are four options on the left side of the dialog box: Output, Marks And Bleeds, PostScript Options, and Color Management.

6 Select Output, and then choose Separations from the Color menu.

7 Click the Ink Manager button in the Ink Manager area.

8 In the Ink Manager dialog box, select the icon to the left of the TOYO 0349 name. The icon changes into a CMYK color swatch, indicating that this color will be printed as a process color, using the cyan, magenta, yellow, and black plates.

Acrobat will mix cyan and black to simulate the dedicated ink that is used to produce the TOYO 0349 spot color. In many cases, it is more cost-effective to use a mixture of CMYK inks than to add an entirely new spot color ink.

To globally convert all spot colors to their CMYK equivalents, select Convert All Spots To Process.

9 Click OK to close the Ink Manager dialog box.

10 In the Advanced Print Setup dialog box, select Marks And Bleeds from the list on the left. Select All Marks to enable trim marks, bleed marks, registration marks, color bars, and page information to print on each plate, outside the edges of the document.

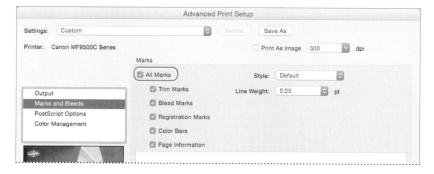

Note: If you've chosen a printer that does not support CMYK printing, the Working CMYK profile will not be available in the Color Profile menu. In that case, choose the Working RGB profile instead.

11 Select Color Management from the list on the left.

12 Choose Acrobat Color Management from the Color Handling menu.

13 Choose Working CMYK: U.S. Web Coated (SWOP) v2 from the Color Profile menu.

The color profile you select should match the device you will be printing to.

14 Click Save As at the top of the Advanced Print Setup dialog box, and save your settings using the name **Profile**. Then click OK.

Saved settings are added to the settings menu, so you can reuse them for future print jobs without having to re-enter the settings for recurring publications or specific output devices.

15 Click OK to exit the Advanced Print Setup dialog box. Then either click OK to print this document, or click Cancel if you prefer not to print at this time.

16 Close the document, and quit Acrobat.

Review questions

1 What is a PDF preset?

2 How can you select a settings file when you create a PDF using the Print command in Mac OS?

3 What problems can Preflight detect within a PDF?

4 What is a spot color, and how can you remap it to a process color when you print color separations?

Review answers

1 A PDF preset is a group of settings that affects the process of creating a PDF file. These settings are designed to balance file size with quality, depending on how the PDF file will be used.

2 To change the settings file in Mac OS, first choose Save As Adobe PDF from the PDF menu in the Print dialog box. Then choose a preset from the Adobe PDF Settings menu.

3 Use the Preflight command to check for all areas of concern within a PDF. For example, if you are sending a PDF file to a professional printer, preflight the document to verify that fonts are embedded, graphics have the appropriate resolution, and colors are correct.

4 A spot color is a special premixed ink that is used instead of, or in addition to, CMYK process inks, and that requires its own printing plate on a printing press. If absolute color accuracy is not critical, and it is not practical to print a spot color plate as well as CMYK plates, you can remap the spot color to a process color for printing using the Ink Manager. In the Advanced Print Setup dialog box, select Separations, and then click Ink Manager. In the Ink Manager, click the icon to the left of the spot color to remap it to a process color for the print job.

INDEX

highlighting areas affected by transparency 268

Highlight Text tool 202, 205

Home screen 12

I

image-editing application, using to edit images in a PDF 120

images

adding 118

converting to PDF 36

copying 121–123

cropping 119

editing in Acrobat 117–120

editing in another application 120

exporting from Acrobat 121–122

replacing 117

saving 122

importing

actions 256

comments 208

preflight profiles 266

initial view, setting to Full Screen mode 28

Initial View tab in the Document Properties dialog box 107

Ink Manager 274, 276

inserting

blank pages 44

images 118

pages from one PDF file into another 94

Insert Pages dialog box 44

Insert Text tool 202, 206

inspecting objects in a PDF file 275

installers, Acrobat Reader 12

installing Acrobat 2

instruction steps, adding to actions 248

interactive forms, creating 220

Internet settings, for converting web pages 53

inviting reviewers 212

K

keyboard shortcuts 83

keywords, adding to a PDF 107

L

labels, adding to form fields 227

Larger File Size option in the Combine Files dialog box 157

layers, printing 265

layout of forms 222

learning resources 4

lesson files, downloading 3

Line Art And Text Resolution option 271

Link Properties dialog box 100

links

adding actions to 100

changing the destination of 100

creating 101

editing 100

list boxes, adding to forms 229

list, display contents of Combine Files dialog box as 157

listing comments 208, 209

LiveCycle Rights Management 167

logos in digital signatures 184

M

magnification

  about 62

  changing 15, 19

magnifying glass in the Combine Files dialog box 151

mail merge, converting Word files to PDF 138

Make Accessible action 78–80

Make Searchable option 51

malicious files, preventing damage from 164

Manage Actions dialog box 256

markup tools 202–203

Marquee Zoom tool 65

menu bar, reopening 13

merging files into a single PDF 146–161

metadata, adding to PDF files 107

Microsoft Excel

  exporting tables to 127

  using PDFMaker with 138–142

Microsoft Office applications, using PDFMaker with 132–145

Microsoft Office files, including in combined files 148

Microsoft Office for Mac OS, creating PDFs from 39

Microsoft PowerPoint

  exporting presentations to 123

  using PDFMaker with 143–144

Microsoft SharePoint, using to distribute forms 233

Microsoft Word documents

  converting with PDFMaker 133–138

  saving PDF files as 125

Microsoft WordPad, creating PDF files from 46

minus sign in the Combine Files dialog box 153

mobile app for Acrobat DC 6, 11

monitor resolution 62

movie files, adding to a PDF 106

moving

  pages 92

  text bounding boxes 116

multiline text fields, adding 223

multimedia files, adding to PDF files 106

multiple documents

  combining into a single PDF 40

  viewing 24

N

naming

  form fields 222

  radio buttons 225

navigating

  documents 62–70

  in Full Screen mode 27

  PDF files 19, 62

  with Enter and Return keys 63

  with scroll bar 64

Navigation Bar in Full Screen mode 27

navigation pane 90

  Page Thumbnails panel 20

  Security Settings button in 167

  Signatures panel 191

  Tags panel 78

navigation tools, adding to the toolbar 66

New Bookmark button 23, 105

Next Page button 23

Next Page command 20

Next View button 67

proofing onscreen 275

properties

    document 107

    editing for form fields 223

Protected Mode in Acrobat Reader 11

    disabling 11

    verifying 164–165

protecting PDF files 166–197

Protect tool 18, 169

Q

Quick Tools on toolbar

    customizing 30

R

radio buttons

    adding 225, 229

    naming 225

rasterization 269

Raster/Vector Balance slider 270

reading

    comments 208

    PDFs 62

reading out loud 83

Reading preferences 83–84

Read mode 29–30

rearranging pages in a PDF 92

Recognition Report 81

Record Audio tool 203

Rectangle tool 203

redacting text 117

Redact tool 117

reducing file size 48

reflowing

    a PDF file 77–79

    text 113

remapping spot colors to process colors 274, 276

Remove Selected Items button in the Combine Files dialog box 41

Remove Split command 26

removing pages from combined files 153

renumbering pages 97–99

reopening the menu bar 13

Replace Text tool 202, 206

replacing

    images 117

    multiple occurrences of text 113

    text 113–114

replying to comments 211

Require A Password To Open The Document option 170

resampling 49, 50

reset buttons, adding to forms 226

resetting toolbars 67

resizing

    form fields 223

    text bounding boxes 116

resolution, checking 275

resources for learning Acrobat 4

response file, adding form data to 234

Results pane in the Preflight dialog box 264–265

Return key, navigating with 63

reversing digital signatures 193

reviewers, inviting to an email-based review 212

Production Notes

Adobe Acrobat DC Classroom in a Book was created electronically using Adobe InDesign CC (2014 release). Art was produced using Adobe InDesign, Adobe Illustrator, and Adobe Photoshop.

References to company names in the lessons are for demonstration purposes only and are not intended to refer to any actual organization or person.

Images

Photographic images and illustrations are intended for use with the tutorials.

Typefaces used

Adobe Myriad Pro and Adobe Minion Pro are used throughout the lessons. For more information about OpenType and Adobe fonts, visit www.adobe.com/type/opentype/.

Team credits

The following individuals contributed to the development of *Adobe Acrobat DC Classroom in a Book*:

Writer: Brie Gyncild

Project Manager: Lisa Fridsma

Lesson Development: Brie Gyncild

Illustrator and Compositor: Lisa Fridsma

Copyeditor and Proofreader: Wendy Katz

Technical Reviewer: Megan Ahearn

Indexer: Brie Gyncild

Cover design: Eddie Yuen

Interior design: Mimi Heft

Adobe Press Executive Editor: Victor Gavenda

Adobe Press Project Editor: Tracey Croom

LEARN BY VIDEO

Learn by Video is a critically acclaimed training series that offers exceptional quality high-definition video to teach the most essential creative technologies and topics. Experienced instructors and industry professionals present hours of video tutorials, complete with lesson files, assessment quizzes, and review materials.

Available in DVD and streaming formats.

To see a full list of titles go to
www.learnbyvideo.com

Add bookmarks in your video for later reference

Lesson files are included

Up to 13 hours of high-quality video training

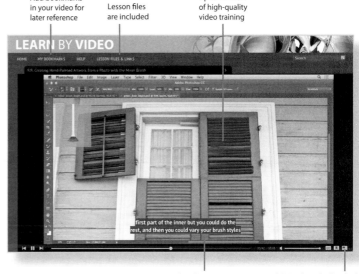

Closed Captioning option available

Watch & Work mode shrinks the video into a small window while you work in the software

Titles

The Photographer's Workflow: Adobe Lightroom 5 and Adobe Photoshop CC
ISBN: 9780321984227

Adobe Photoshop Lightroom 5 Learn by Video
ISBN: 9780133902648

Adobe Photoshop CC Learn by Video (2014 release)
ISBN: 9780133927726

Adobe Illustrator CC Learn by Video (2014 release)
ISBN: 9780133928068

Adobe InDesign CC Learn by Video (2014 release)
ISBN: 9780133928075

Adobe Dreamweaver CC Learn by Video (2014 release)
ISBN: 9780133928099

Adobe Flash Professional CC Learn by Video (2014 release)
ISBN: 9780133928105

Adobe Premiere Pro CC Learn by Video (2014 release)
ISBN: 9780133928105

Adobe After Effects CC Learn by Video (2014 release)
ISBN: 9780133928266

Peachpit

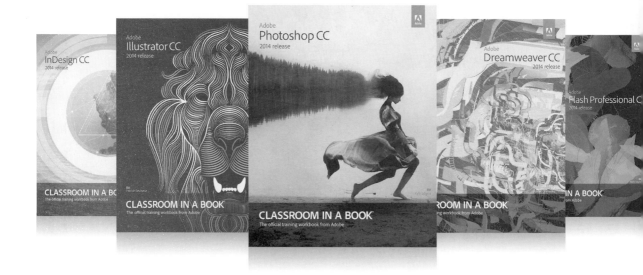

The fastest, easiest, most comprehensive way to learn
Adobe® Creative Cloud™

Classroom in a Book®, the best-selling series of hands-on software training books, helps you learn the features of Adobe software quickly and easily.

The **Classroom in a Book** series offers what no other book or training program does—an official training series from Adobe Systems, developed with the support of Adobe product experts.

To see a complete list of our Adobe Creative Cloud titles go to:
www.adobepress.com/adobecc2014

Adobe Photoshop CC Classroom in a Book (2014 release)
ISBN: 9780133924442

Adobe Illustrator CC Classroom in a Book (2014 release)
ISBN: 9780133905656

Adobe InDesign CC Classroom in a Book (2014 release)
ISBN: 9780133904390

Adobe Muse CC Classroom in a Book (2014 release) *eBook Only
ISBN: 9780133854145

Adobe Dreamweaver CC Classroom in a Book (2014 release)
ISBN: 9780133924404

Adobe Flash Professional CC Classroom in a Book (2014 release)
ISBN: 9780133927108

Adobe Premiere Pro CC Classroom in a Book (2014 release)
ISBN: 9780133927054

Adobe After Effects CC Classroom in a Book (2014 release)
ISBN: 9780133927030

Adobe**Press**